Without a Thorn

WITHOUT A THORN

A Guide to Rose Gardening in the Pacific Northwest

**Stuart Mechlin
and Ellen Bonanno**

Timber Press   **Forest Grove, Oregon**

For our parents

Library of Congress Catalog Card Number: 78-13890
ISBN: 0-917304-37-3

Printed in the United States of America.

Timber Press
P.O. Box 92
Forest Grove, OR 97116

ACKNOWLEDGMENTS

We would like to thank the following people and organizations for their invaluable help in preparing this book. Our three friends and associates most closely involved with the production of this book are: John Jackson, whose clear and precise illustrations greatly enhance our text; Larry Jones, whose photographs illustrate the beauty of the rose in many settings; and Dick Abel, our editor, whose astute comments helped clarify and polish our prose.

We would also like to thank Henry and Mary Jorgensen and Terrence O'Donnell for their early encouragement when the thought of writing this book seemed a remote dream.

Rodger Larson, Landscape Designer, has been of great help in forming and shaping our ideas on landscaping with roses.

We are particularly indebted to Fred and Wini Edmunds, of "Roses by Fred Edmunds," for their rose growing advice over the years, and their friendship.

Our thanks to *Horticulture* magazine for allowing us to use material first published in their pages.

We are indebted to the Portland Bureau of Parks and Recreation for maintaining a number of very beautiful public rose gardens, one of which one of the authors has had the opportunity of working in.

A special note of thanks to Ron Rau, who started us growing roses.

We have also been fortunate in being associated with one of the finest groups of amateur rose growers in the United States, the Portland Rose Society, a talented and diverse group whose members give of themselves tirelessly to promote rose growing in the Portland area.

The following people have graciously allowed us to take photographs of their lovely rose gardens: Mrs. Harvey Barragar; Mr. and Mrs. Fred Edmunds; Mrs. J.R. Fullerton; Mrs. Ellen Magette; Mr. and Mrs. Joseph Mozena; Miss AnnaJo Ness; Mr. and Mrs. Walter Regan; Mrs. James P. Smith; and Mr. and Mrs. Harry West.

Finally, for deciphering, typing and commenting, we extend our heartfelt appreciation to two top professionals, Gayle Larson and Joyce Chambers.

CONTENTS

MINIATURE ROSES   65

DISPLAYING AND SHOWING YOUR ROSES   73

APPENDIX

INTRODUCTION

We like roses. We like to see the pleasure on people's faces when they are given a bouquet or admire some well-grown bushes in a friend's garden. We like to see that glow of pride and joy in people who grow roses, who know they have created beauty where there was little before. We marvel and wonder at all the different colors of roses and color changes as the buds open and bloom. We are amazed at how many different sizes and shapes of blooms and bushes there can be.

We like roses in the spring before they flower because with each warm day you can see the new red shoots grow and expand with the sun. We like them in the summer because of all the fragrance that exudes from the blossoms on a hot day. We like them best of all in the fall when the weather is rainy and cold, and all we can look forward to is the winter; but there are still roses to cut and bring into the house to enjoy and remind us of summer. Roses, because of their long growing season, color, fragrance, different sizes and shapes and their almost perfect adaptation to the climate of the Pacific Northwest, give you so much more than any other flower or plant you can grow here. This book is an attempt to show you how to grow and enjoy them at their best.

This book is for you, the gardener who only has a few roses and wants to grow them better, or who is thinking about planting some and is not really sure just what to do. Roses, like any plant, do need specific care and attention, even though they grow well in our climate. We are going to show you how to get the best return and results from your investment of time and energy in the care of your roses. The information presented here addresses itself to the most asked questions and problems of new and unskilled Pacific Northwest rose growers.

The first chapter gives you ideas on how and where to use roses around your home. Next we deal with a subject that stops many from growing roses—how to select and buy (and get the most for your money), and how to plant them to insure success. Then, using a seasonal approach, we provide a complete guide to rose care. So while this chapter starts with the spring season you may pick up the thread at any point depending on which season you need the information, as it is all related in a cycle. Following the chapter on care, we provide a chapter on the very versatile miniature roses which will be of special interest to those who only have a small space in which to garden.

Roses invoke such a great wealth of feeling that not long after you start growing them, you want to show them to others. Our chapter on displaying roses both at home and at a rose show tells you how to do both. Lastly, the appendices give you such information as our favorite varieties, how to identify insects and diseases and a list of public rose gardens in the Pacific Northwest.

This book will be as handy to you as your pruning shears. It will help you grow your roses well, be they many or few, and most importantly, to enjoy them fully.

LANDSCAPING WITH ROSES

How fortunate you are to have an outdoor area, be it a balcony
or half-acre, in which to place and enjoy roses, plants and other
outdoor fixtures in any way you wish. In this chapter we are going
to give you ideas and guidelines about using roses which will
enable you to look at your own area and expand the possibilities.
There are so many different lot sizes and shapes; home sizes and
shapes; and compatible plant varieties that to be specific and try to
cover every possible problem with hard and fast rules would leave
you dissatisfied because you always seem to have a unique spot
that has not been covered. Instead you will find that the general
ideas we discuss here: cultural requirements; design ideas; and
lastly, specific outdoor areas that are common to all gardens, will
allow you to adapt roses in many ways to your particular site.

CULTURAL REQUIREMENTS

You want your roses to grow well, so there are a few important
cultural considerations to keep in mind when deciding where to
plant that will affect the life and health of the bushes. First, roses
need a good half day or more of sun to bloom well; second, they
like to have their roots in well-drained soil; and third, they prefer
it if the other plant competition is separated by a little distance.

These factors are not as restrictive as they seem. Light intensity
depends on many factors such as exposure—south instead of
north; or reflected light from sidewalks, decks, lightly colored

walls or fences, which may provide the plants with enough light in what otherwise is a poor spot. Giving rose roots well-drained soil is as easy as improving the soil with amendments or raising the rose bed a few inches to promote drainage. Three or four feet (hardly noticeable when you have vigorous roses and vigorous surrounding plants) is all roses need to have some ground to call their own.

DESIGN CONSIDERATIONS

Keeping the above guidelines in mind, there are other aspects about planting roses which do not affect the health of the plants but are worth thinking about. These are the design considerations, or how the plants will look in their setting.

Roses, like fine paintings, make their best appearance when framed. The vibrancy of the leaves and the colors of the blooms need a frame to set them off. A frame can be anything from a background of evergreens to a brick walkway or a green lawn in front of the planting. Such settings do an excellent job of highlighting rose bushes, especially in the spring when the new foliage is so red. The muted earth tones of a concrete walk, wood deck or wood fence will perform a similar function. These edges, borders, and frames give the rose planting definition and form which heighten your appreciation of the colors and blooms. For this reason, rose plantings in containers always look good because the container is a natural frame that highlights the plants.

As with most colorful plants, roses like to be planted with other roses to give a mass effect whose sum is always greater than the parts alone. Single bushes of many different varieties in one area will give a very uneven appearance to your rose beds due to the different heights and growth habits of each plant. Consider this when deciding where to place them. Choose a spot which can hold three plants or more of one color. A single rose bush placed to simply fill in a spot rarely looks well. If you want many colors, plant individual varieties in grouped color blocks. If you are after a kaleidoscope effect, plant a mass bed of one of the many varieties that change color as the flower buds open.

OUTDOOR USE AREAS

With these landscaping guidelines in mind, you may have visualized new ways and areas in which to plant roses. Even more importantly, by understanding the effects of frames and color blocks you now know why you have liked rose plantings that you have seen in other yards or in public gardens and how to duplicate that pleasing effect around your home. However, in order to realize these specific principles in the outdoor spaces available to you, you must be able to apply them in your specific location.

To help you in applying these principles to your specific space, we will now look at the three uses common to nearly every home: the private outdoor living room; the entryway; and functional elements such as fences, screens and walkways. These areas are not distinct in a real landscape but by looking at your outdoor area in terms of these sections you will be able to plan what kind of roses you want and where you want them before you buy.

Perhaps the most important area in the landscape is the outdoor living room, that section of the garden that you actively use alone or with family and friends to relax and enjoy the warm months of the year. Roses, unlike other plants which bloom sporadically or only in one season, are in bloom during the entire time you are outside enjoying the summer. If your area is large and the viewpoint extensive, larger growing and larger flowering hybrid teas and grandifloras should be planted to keep the landscaping in proportion to the space. If your space and view are limited, either by design or surrounding homes and lots, floribundas provide the appropriate scale and won't overpower you when viewed from close by.

Roses can be planted alongside your patio, deck, or lawn area where you spend most of your time. Very fragrant roses are especially suitable and attractive here.

Sometimes, a little mystery is needed in the landscape, so planting roses in a spot partially blocked from view by other garden features heightens your enjoyment as you come upon them while working or walking around the garden. Roses can also be used to highlight certain areas in the garden that you particularly like such as a small pool, sundial, or birdfeeder, much as you would highlight a table in your indoor living room with a vase of flowers.

The next area of importance for any home is the entryway, where visitors get their first impression of you, your family and your home. Roses used here direct people to the front door and invite them in by acting as a beacon with their bright colors. A planting of fragrant roses near the door will entertain guests during the few moments they wait.

The fragrance will also enter the house everytime you open the door for any reason. The entryway is where you enter your home after being away for any length of time. Seeing blooming roses from a short distance away before you actually get there adds one more ingredient to the affection we all feel for where we live.

Remember, the space available here is usually small and restricted. The entry is also low on the list in relation to the time you have to spend on garden chores. Low growing floribundas, especially some of the newer disease resistant types, are a good choice for this spot.

Lastly, you can plant roses where their beauty can enhance a functional requirement. Roses and fences or other privacy barriers work well together whether the idea is to hide or enhance the fence. Nothing is uglier or more secure than a chain link fence. Unfortunately it affords little privacy. Climbing roses trained on the fence as well as tall growing roses planted in front of it are a natural choice to hide the ugly aspects of the fence and block undesirable views. Some fences of cedar or redwood are attractive in themselves but even here roses can liven up what is essentially a straight line.

It is best to stay with one variety or alternate a few varieties consistently when planting along fences. The formal lines of the fence are emphasized and reinforced when the planting pattern is repeated to create a uniform and complete barrier.

Roses planted along walkways are useful in that their thorns will keep people on the walkways and away from areas you don't want them to go.

Today many people are creating functional privacy screens with evergreens that are also naturalized settings. Evergreens, used informally or formally as screens, include conifers such as cedar and spruce or broad-leaf shrubs such as rhododendrons, all of which make a good backdrop for framing roses. Even where you are trying for a woodsy style or effect with many natural and native-looking plants and a background of pines or firs, roses will work. There are many roses that have single open flowers and foliage that is glossy like the native huckleberry. These single types blend well with native plant material. You only have to travel through a Pacific Northwest valley forest and see our native wild roses growing among the oaks and firs to realize how well roses look and grow with native plants. The softer colors of the single types lend a variety to the naturalized landscape and yet blend well with the forest palette.

The last way to look at where to plant your roses is the view that you create for yourself from inside your home. Even though roses are blooming when you can be outside to enjoy them, you cannot be outside all the time, so how they look from the inside becomes important too. Your windows are the frames for living outdoor pictures. Before planting roses for any of the above reasons step back into the house and imagine what it will look like from there. You will find that a whole new diminsion is added and perhaps by moving a planting a few feet or adding a planting your enjoyment can be increased.

CLASSIFICATION OF ROSE TYPES

We are ending this chapter with our classification of rose plants to further help you in buying and placing them around your home. Our classifications are based both on the official system of the American Rose Society all the major rose growers use combined with the way we have observed roses growing in the Pacific Northwest.

Hybrid Teas and Grandifloras

These bushes grow from four to six feet tall. They produce large multipetalled (double) flowers although there are a few open single flowers in this classification. In our climate these roses can produce either one very large pointed flower to a stem or clusters of somewhat smaller flowers on one stem. If you want to insure one rose on a long stem you have to pinch out the side flower buds below the main flower bud. The clusters of flowers are excellent where you need a large mass of color. These roses should be planted between two-and-a-half and three-and-a-half feet apart. The difference between Hybrid Teas and Grandifloras is very arbitrary and there are more differences within each classification than between them.

Floribundas

Floribundas grow from two to four feet high. The flowers are small and numerous. They can either grow in clusters of up to 20 on one stem or individual flowers on single stems. Flower form ranges from singles to very double types. The individual flowers in the clusters open up separately, creating color effect lasting over a long period of time. The growth habit of these bushes ranges from very low and compact to open and rangy. They should be planted two to three feet apart.

Climbers

Roses that grow long canes of at least six feet and can be trained on a support are climbers. The color range and flower form vary widely. Because of the need for vegetative growth, climbers usually take two seasons or more to flower well.

Miniatures

Miniatures are low growing (usually one foot tall) plants with truly tiny flowers. Some minis will have canes up to two feet tall, as tall as some floribundas, but you can't mistake the miniature foliage and flowers of these plants.

Shrub Roses

Shrub roses are large bush type plants with many arching and branching canes coming from the base. These will usually flower once in early summer and only sporadically after that. They will get quite large and rangy as the summer progresses.

This is a colorful and striking solution to a difficult problem: a sloping and uneven front yard hemmed in on one side by a large building. The red and white masses of color successfully meet the challenge.

Roses go well with modern architecture and the weathered look of unstained wood.

These Red Devils are show bloom quality and yet form a unified landscape element in the garden.

What an inviting way to look for someone's front door! The owner has created an atmosphere that will give pleasure to everyone who walks through this garden from the street.

These two varieties of roses planted together provide a contrast in flower form, while giving you unity in color.

This mass planting of just two roses—Memorium and Audie Murphy—proves that a simple idea can make even a driveway a feast for the eye.

These roses thrive in the partial shade of this tree.

These climbers complement the classic lines of this older home and create a distinctive entryway.

A complete garden of roses in two small redwood planter boxes.

The modern lines of this fence provide a dramatic backdrop for this Royal Gold climber when viewed from inside the house; it is actually planted on the street side of the fence.

This climbing Dortmund has been trained and pruned correctly to bloom profusely.

These lower growing floribundas are in perfect scale with this small patio and make this an even more pleasant place to enjoy the summer weather.

The floribunda City of Belfast leads you right to the front door.

These roses are framed 2 ways: in front by the lawn and behind by the conifer hedge.

A simple, low-maintenance solution to highlighting an entryway—a mass planting of Sarabandes framed by a green lawn and a row of camellias.

These floribundas highlight this small birdbath and tie it in with the rest of the garden.

BUYING AND PLANTING ROSES

BUYING ROSES

Roses can be purchased in many forms and types of packaging over a long season, from mid-December until July. The dormant rose plant, with moderate care, has very good keeping qualities which permits it to be sold and packaged in a variety of ways. If you know how to handle each type of package and what to expect from it you can choose among them intelligently.

Bareroot Roses

Bareroot roses are freshly-dug, dormant plants that are stored and shipped without any soil around the roots. Plants are dug in November and December and immediately put in moist, cold storage warehouses until they are shipped, either directly to you from a mail-order rose nursery or to a local retail nursery. The storage and shipping system is very sophisticated and there is almost no chance of the plants either drying out or getting damaged between digging and final destination. These roses are handled less than any other type of roses you can buy and consequently are healthier and will establish themselves faster in your garden. You may be apprehensive about ordering through the mail, but buying from any of the large mail-order firms specializing in roses is really the best way to buy. These firms will ship your roses at the correct planting time for your area. They ship only number one grade roses (see Section on Grading in this

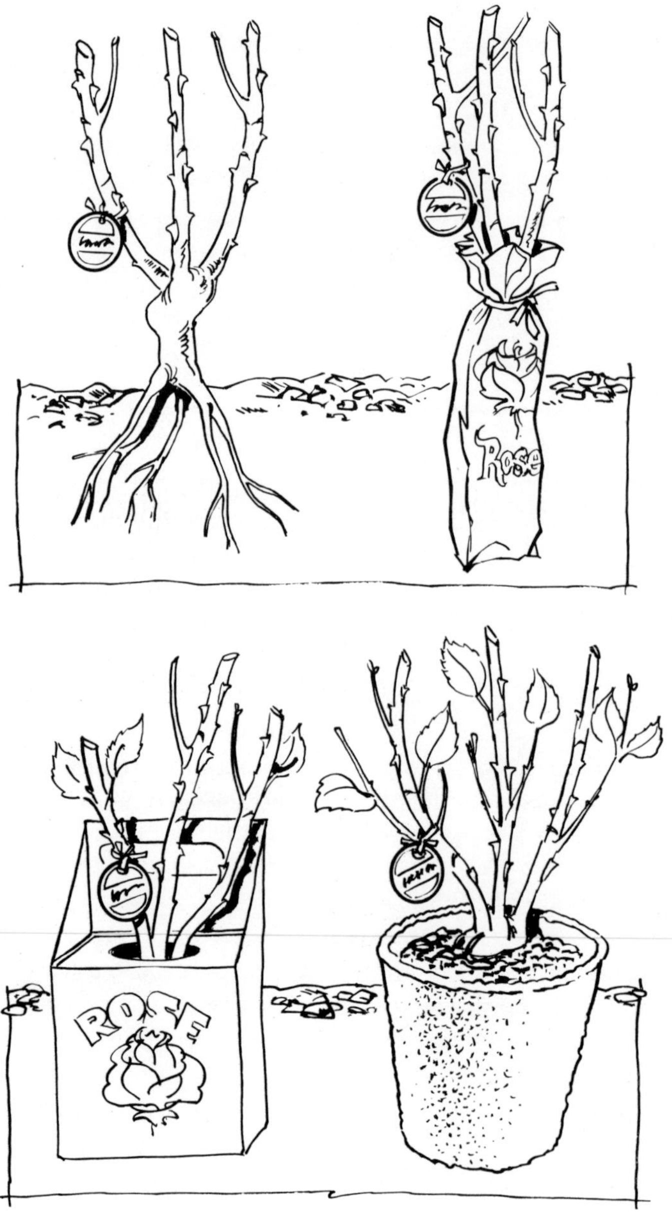

1. The four main ways roses are sold are: bareroot, foil-wrapped, plantable-box, and potted.

chapter for explanation). They usually have the latest introductions and although their prices are not inexpensive, the initial investment pays off in years of good growth and flowers. These firms also have a replacement policy for bushes that fail to grow the first year.

If you buy your bareroot roses from a local retail nursery, be sure that they have been protected from frost and drying out by being kept in a moist mulch such as barkdust or sawdust. Before you buy, check both roots and canes for signs of drying out such as black roots and shrivelled or brownish canes.

Foil-Wrapped Roses

Foil-wrapped or packaged roses are the most inexpensive and convenient way to buy. The roots of the freshly dug roses are cut to a uniform length; wrapped in damp moss or sawdust; and placed in a foil and plastic wrapper. The protruding canes are coated with a protective wax to inhibit drying out. There is usually a picture of the rose pasted on the package. These plants are not apt to get off to as good a start as bareroot plants because more handling means more potential damage to the roots and canes either from breakage or drying out. In addition, the longer they sit on the store shelf the less desirable they become. The packaged rose plant cannot be watered easily, so the roots are in danger of drying out. They are usually stacked in an open area and hence subject to rapid temperature changes which may cause damage to the delicate root tips.

However, these plants are a good buy because of their lower price. They should be purchased immediately after the store has received them from the grower in February and March. Don't be afraid to ask the store manager when they arrived. Do not buy foil-wrapped rose bushes later than the end of March. Bought early and given good care, these plants will start slowly, but should grow and flower as well as any other roses after one season. These roses are sold both in number one grade and number one-and-a-half grade (see Section on Grading), so if you are comparing prices be sure you are comparing the same grade.

Potted Roses

Potted roses are bareroot rose plants that haven't sold and are potted up in May by the garden center before they start to grow vigorously. In order to promote root growth through good aeration and moisture retention the soil mix should be light and porous. A slow release fertilizer is usually added to keep the plant growing well all summer. Potted roses, like any potted shrub, can be bought and planted any time during the summer, although the best time to buy these plants is in June and July. A good nursery will take proper care of these plants, making sure they are watered, sprayed and fertilized, but by the end of July they may be getting root bound; disease problems grow dramatically due to crowding; and it is difficult for the nursery to keep the roots sufficiently wet in the summer heat. The great advantage of potted roses is that good roses can be purchased as late as early summer so you can see exactly what the color and size of the bloom is and not rely on pictures or descriptions in a catalogue.

Plantable-Box Roses

The newest method of selling and packaging roses is the plantable-box rose. Though more expensive than foil-wrapped roses, the plantable-box has received enthusiastic response from many garden center operators because it provides an attractive display and is easier to maintain in fresh condition than either foil-wrapped or bareroot roses. This new package consists of a pruned, number one grade waxed rose in a carton made of heavy water-resistant cardboard and filled with a sterile planting media. The carton is designed to be placed in the ground with a minimum of handling and to gradually decompose. It comes with a carrying handle, and is properly labelled. Extensive directions accompany the box which can be stored and displayed inside or outside the store.

For the novice rose grower a plantable box has some definite advantages. It can be stored as long as the soil medium is kept moist. Openings around the paper collar at the top of the package make watering easier during storage. The uniform media in the package are formulated to provide drainage and aeration; promote good root growth; and includes a small amount of slow-release fertilizer that will not burn the growing root tips. This type of packaging is a successful attempt to eliminate some of the major problems associated with foil-wrapping yet at the same time providing a convenient method to get the roses off to as good a start as bareroot roses. Even though plantable-box roses do store well at the nursery, they should not be purchased past the end of May. They are not as easy to plant as the directions on the package imply but by following our special instructions in the planting section they will establish themselves better than foil-wrapped roses.

Buying Versus Home Propagation

Commercially grown roses are a merger of two types of plants: a strong rootstock developed specifically for fast root growth; and a rose variety developed for its unique color and form. The different named varieties are budded (a type of grafting) onto the rootstock to form the complete plants. The budded plants are grown for two years at the rose nursery before being sold to you. The budding process requires great skill and experience to perform successfully.

Another method, not used commercially, is to root cuttings of rose canes. These plants are not as strong as budded plants and do not produce a good quantity or quality of blooms. Furthermore, the percentage of cuttings that will actually root is small.

We do not recommend home propagation of roses as a way to expand your garden. Home propagation can be very frustrating to the home gardener since the success rate is low both in the plants you are able to propagate and their quality. Your time and energy will be better utilized in buying, planting and growing intelligently. If your finances are limited, the best rose buy for the money are fresh foil-wrapped roses that are sold at sale prices in late February and early March.

Grading—What it Means

There are two reasons in addition to packaging which explain why some roses cost more than others—grade and variety. Where they are grown matters very little since most are grown in a climate well suited for production of a strong plant, such as California, Texas and Oregon. The rootstocks used by all the rose growers are selected to be hardy in all areas of the country.

After the dormant roses are dug they are graded. There are three grades used. Number one grade is a rose bush consisting of three or four, one-half-inch-thick canes. Number one-and-a-half grade has two or three canes of smaller diameter. Number two grade is a very weak plant with perhaps one good cane and few roots, and which most growers consign to the burn pile. Most mail-order rose firms ship number one grade only. Foil-wrapped roses are usually either number one or number one-and-a-half grade. (Be sure to note the grade that is marked on the package when comparing prices.) Number one roses have a lot of energy reserves in the canes and roots to start producing many flowers and much foliage immediately. One-and-a-half grade is a good buy if fresh because of its price, but be prepared to wait two seasons before they really start producing many quality blooms.

New varieties are usually more expensive than older ones because of the initial expense of developing, patenting and promoting the rose by the originating rose company. Most rose growers maintain expensive research facilities dedicated to developing new combinations of colors and fragrance which will attract the rose buyer. The very newness of the rose variety is also a factor in pricing as new roses are produced in limited quantities and are usually popular simply because they are new. Newness does not necessarily imply better. While it is true that there have been great advances in disease resistance, color and fragrance which only a few years ago was thought impossible, many excellent older varieties are still available. In addition, older varieties whose patents have expired are usually one or two dollars cheaper for the same grade and quality of rose plant.

Storing Roses

Planning is the key to planting roses. If the ground and layout of the rose bed is prepared *before* you buy, the quicker the plants will be in the ground and the better they will do. But many times weather and other commitments prohibit you from getting everything ready before you receive or buy your roses, so it will be necessary to store them at your home for a short time.

If your bareroot roses have come in the mail, open the carton to air them out and re-moisten the plants. Also check that your order is correct as speed is essential if adjustments are necessary. Plants can be stored in the carton for a week at the most.

Remove foil-wrapped roses from their wrappers and moisten before you store them. If you have to store bareroot or foil-wrapped roses for any length of time, put them in a cool, damp place with the roots and tops covered by a damp mulch-like barkdust. Leave potted and plantable-box roses in their containers and keep damp. An unheated basement, garage or an outside location protected from the wind is ideal. Storing roses for longer than a month, particularly bareroot and foil-wrapped types, weakens the plants and makes them that much harder to establish.

PLANTING

Laying the groundwork for any endeavor is a sure ingredient for success. With roses you can take this phrase quite literally, as preparing the actual ground you will plant in and planting them correctly are the two key factors in addition to buying intelligently which will insure lasting rose growing success.

Soil Preparation

The environment that you put your rose roots in, the soil, is more mysterious than the outside environment around the leaves and flowers. Except for the surface, you can't see what is going on in the soil, and changes there are not as dramatic as above ground. Yet the structure and texture of the earth around the roots, if prepared well, will help your roses more than any other care you can give them. Good soil promotes good root growth which makes plants bigger and stronger and enables them to withstand droughts as well as waterlogged conditions and freezes. *Before* you plant is the only time, short of digging up and re-planting, when you can get down deep into the soil and make the necessary textural and structural changes with soil amendments.

When you have decided where you are going to put your roses, look at and feel the soil to find out what type it is. Most soils in the Pacific Northwest are clay types, but there are many sandy types in the Puget Sound area and near rivers and streams. Heavy clay soils stay water-logged in the winter and dry and crack in the summer discouraging fibrous root tips so important for good plant growth. Sandy soils drain rapidly in the summer leading to plant stress due to lack of water and leaching of nutrients, which quickly starves the plant.

What you are looking for is a soil somewhere between these two extremes with a bias toward the clay loam type of soil. A simple test to determine the quality of your soil can be performed by squeezing a small amount of damp soil in you hand. If the soil ball squishes together like modeling clay and is hard to break apart, it is too heavy. If it won't stick together at all, it is too loose. If it stays together but small pieces break away when you pick at the soil with your finger, it is just right.

Lucky is the person whose home comes equipped with a loose and friable soil. But lucky are the rest of us because there is a cure which solves all soil structure and texture problems no matter what kind of soil we have. This cure is called organic matter. Organic matter is a soil amendment and not a fertilizer so its principal effect is to improve soil structure and not soil fertility. It not only makes poor soils rich, but good soils better. The chemicals in organic matter and the chemical actions it causes as it decomposes into humus binds up sandy soil and loosens up clay soils. Organic matter also provides a happy environment for earthworms which leave air and water passages in the soil as they move through the ground feeding. Organic matter also promotes the growth of soil micro-organisms which maintain the chemical balance of the soil and so insure that any fertilizers you feed the plants later on will be available to your roses. All these factors enable your rose plant to produce an enormous fibrous root system which means health and vigor for the plant.

The best organic matter available is manure from ruminant animals such as cows, horses, and zoo animals such as elephants. Fresh, rotted or dried manure can be used but at least one month should pass between spading in fresh manure and planting roses so the manure does not damage the root tips of new roses.

Well rotted compost, leaves and peat moss are next on the list of desirable organic matters. Stay away from concentrated organic matter like chicken manure and sawdust both of which do more damage than good and are disagreeable to handle. Barkdust is alright if nothing else is available. Before spading and preparing your new rose bed spread the organic matter evenly on the soil surface. Poor soils should have at least three inches of organic matter added to them; amend better soils with lesser amounts.

The other soil amendment you can add at this time is agricultural lime. Roses like a soil that is a little on the acid side measured on the pH (acidity-alkalinity) scale. The pH for roses should be between 6.1 and 6.8 and can be easily tested with small kits sold at garden centers, or through a state soil test lab. (See Winter Care Section.) If the soil is below 6.1 it can be made less acid by the addition of agricultural lime applied at a rate of ten pounds of lime per 100 square feet. Most soils west of the Cascades tend to be in the acceptable pH range, so the addition of large amounts of lime won't be necessary. Lime also helps break up clay soils and speeds decomposition of the organic matter you add, so you should apply a light covering over the surface of the soil whenever you apply large quantities of organic matter.

You are now ready to spade your soil. The physical action of spading breaks up the soil and aids in drainage and aeration of the soil. Spading also enables you to get your organic matter down deep, twelve inches or more, where the rose roots will eventually be.

Spading is easy to do. Use a round-point shovel with a straight shank for the least strain on your back and the best results in the ground. Push your shovel straight down as far as it will go, bring up the soil and turn the shovel over rapidly, making sure the organic matter is covered by soil. Next jab with the shovel point the soil clod you just dug up to break it into as many small pieces as possible, mixing it with the organic matter at the same time. If your soil is particularly heavy it is easier to spade before applying the organic matter and then spade it again with the organic matter.

The rewards to the rose plant of spading are great, although when faced with a large area, rototilling or rotovating may seem a better idea. You must rototill in the late spring or summer when the soil is dry. If the soil is damp to wet, rototilling does more harm than good, by compacting the soil instead of breaking it apart. Furthermore, a rototiller rarely goes below eight inches, while spading will open the soil twelve inches deep which makes a big difference to the rose plant.

It is important to spade or till as much area as you can without disturbing other plants or permanent features because rose roots fan out at least three feet from the plant itself. Remember again that the more deep, fibrous roots the plant has, the more underground area it can depend on for water and fertilizer during the growing season. After spading, your soil should be fluffy and spongy.

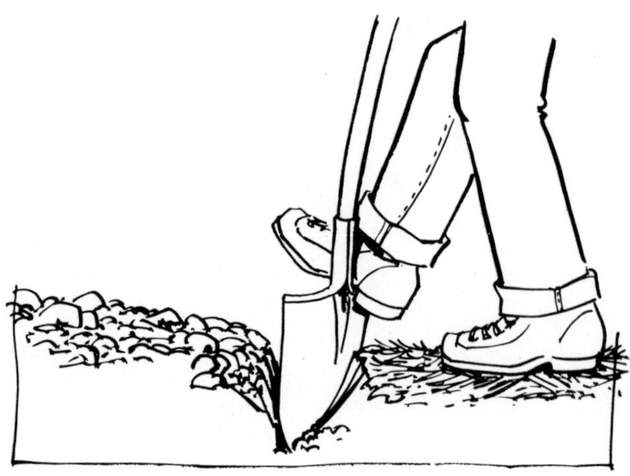

2. When spading always work from spaded soil *backwards* to unspaded soil.

The final step before buying your roses is to stake out the places where each will be planted. Staking will help you get an overall picture of how they will look and permit you to make any necessary spacing changes with stakes rather than plants.

Bareroot and Foil-wrapped Roses

Foil-wrapped roses should be planted as if they were bareroot roses. Both types of plants must be planted between December and March. You can plant them anytime during these months as long as the ground is not frozen and the outside air temperature is above 40 degrees F.

First, no matter what condition the roses are in, soak the roots in room temperature water up to 12 hours, but not more, immediately before planting. This soaking wil insure that the roots are well-filled with water. Then, you should give the roots and tops what we call a "mini-prune." The goal of this pre-planting, mini-pruning is to develop a strong, neat-looking bush which will use its energy as efficiently as possible to produce flowers and stay healthy.

Look at and treat each plant as an individual. Rose bushes vary not only from classification to classification but from variety to variety and from plant to plant of the same grade and variety. The final product should have one to three thick green canes growing up and away from the bud union so the center of the plant is clean and uncluttered. The roots should fan out evenly from the rootstock.

Here's what you should do. Remove any broken canes by cutting below the breaks. Remove any thin, skinny, weak looking or dead canes and stubs by cutting them flush with the bud union or flush with the thicker cane they are growing from. Never cut into the bud union. Check for any crossing canes or two canes growing or rubbing against each other. In each case cut out the weaker of the two. Whenever you prune always work first from the obvious, and then to the discretionary and you can't go wrong. Lastly cut down all the remaining canes to about eight to twelve inches from the bud union using a slanting cut above an outward facing bud eye if possible.

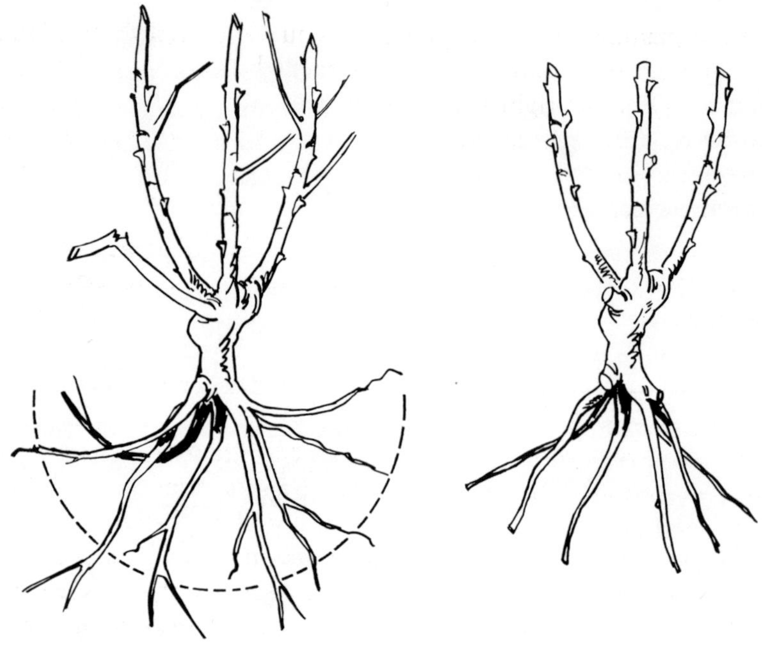

3. Mini prune your new plants by removing all broken, damaged and un-wanted canes and roots.

Next look at the roots. Cut out all roots which are broken, curled or shrivelled. Give all the roots of bareroot roses a clean cut, leaving six to eight inches of roots coming from the rootstock. Even though you are shortening the roots, this cutting has a very important effect. It will promote the growth of many more fibrous roots to reach into the new soil. It is better for the plant to be able to grow these new roots, a process that will start immediately after planting, than for you to attempt to save every existing root by crowding them into the planting hole. With foil-wrapped roses you only have to check for possible broken roots, as the roots have been cut back enough by the grower to get them into the package. You should now have a plant that is neat, cleanly balanced and easy to handle.

Now you are ready to plant your roses. Bring them out to where you will plant them, making sure to keep them damp while you are planting. At the spot where you have decided to plant, remove your stake and dig a hole big enough to accommodate the roots and give the right height to the bud union. The only thing you need add or mix into the hole now is a very *small* handful of bonemeal. Bonemeal doesn't burn the tender new roots and is important for early root growth.

Make a small mound in the center of the hole to support the plant, place it in the hole on the mound, spreading the roots out, and making sure the bud union is at the right height. The bud union should be just above the existing soil line. This exposed position will give you better, and more, new flowering canes. Furthermore, if the bud union or canes are buried under the soil, they form their own roots in the soil. This situation causes the rootstock, which has been chosen for its superior rooting capabilities, to atrophy and die. Put some soil on the roots just to hold the plant in place. Before adding any more soil, again check root spread, bud union height and overall position. Make sure the plant is straight and that it lines up with other plants or your imaginary planting line.

Fill the hole about two-thirds full and check everything again. Water the rose in with a gentle flow until the soil is soggy. The water fills in the air spaces and packs the soil around the roots. Fill the hole up completely, water again, and rake the soil around the bush back to the original level. Check the bud union height one last time. If it is a bit high, *very gently* press the soil around the rose with your foot to lower it. If it is too low, grab the canes with gloved hands and shake and pull the bush *very gently* to the desired height. If you have been checking the height all during the filling process you shouldn't have to raise or lower it at all.

Lastly, mound the newly planted rose with a mulch such as barkdust. Cover the canes to within about one-and-a-half inches at the top to protect the new plants from freezing and drying out. Remove this mound in early May, being careful not to break off any new shoots that have started growing. These shoots will be yellow because of being covered up. They will green up rapidly when exposed to the light.

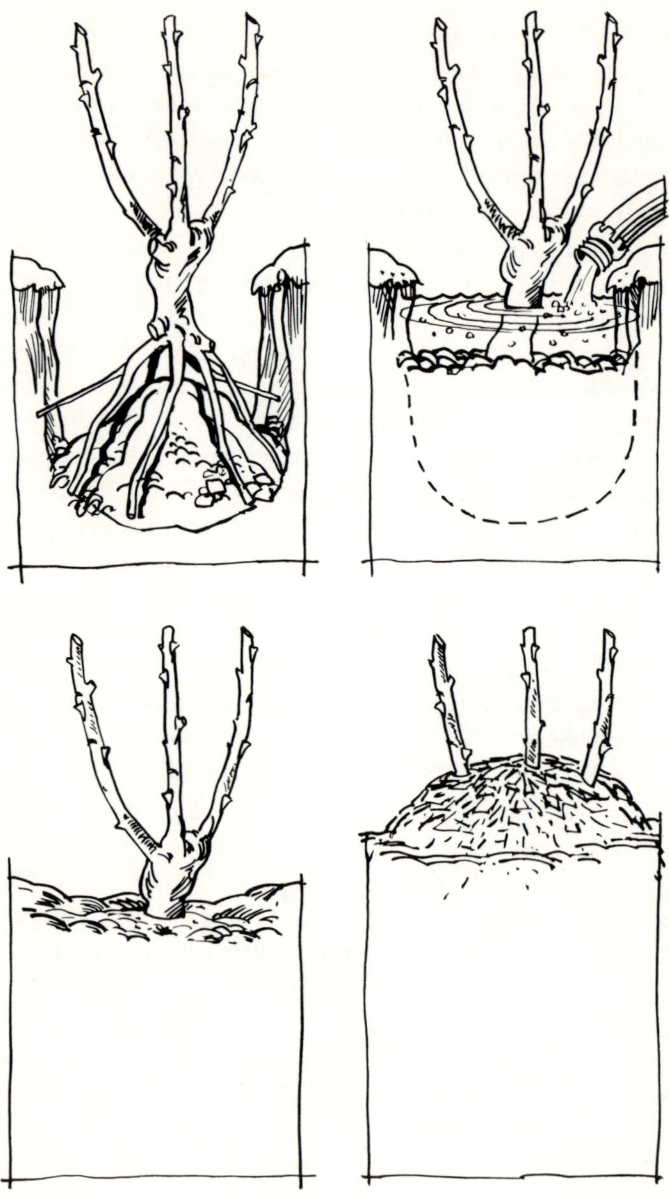

4. The four steps of planting new bareroot and foil-wrapped roses.

Potted Roses

Roses bought in pots are easier to plant than bareroot or foil-wrapped roses. Both the canes and roots have been pruned at the nursery before they were potted up, so except for cutting out any broken canes, the mini-pruning step is eliminated. But, planting potted roses correctly is very important because they are in an actively growing condition.

The potted rose should be watered well before you plant. Measure the pot and dig a hole a bit larger than the pot size and with enough depth to give you the correct bud union height. Set the rose, still in the pot, in the hole to confirm your measurements. Take the pot out of the hole, knock the rose gently out of the pot and place it in the hole. If the bud union height is incorrect you can adjust by adding or removing soil from under the soil ball. Next, gently pull some roots away from the soil ball so they will grow into the surrounding soil with greater ease. Fill the hole with soil, and water in thoroughly as with bareroot roses. You will have soil left over as you have imported new soil with the potted rose, so remove this excess to another area and rake the soil back to its original level. Since potted roses are actively growing and you are planting them in the summer, be very attentive to their water needs in the subsequent weeks and months.

Plantable-Box Roses

Roses in plantable containers can be planted in both the dormant and growing seasons. They are about the easiest of all roses to plant because both the mini-pruning and knocking them out of the pot are eliminated.

Various rose firms use different kinds of packaging so you should read the specific directions for your particular package carefully. In general, however, the essential steps are the same for all packages.

The plants should be damp before you start and any broken canes should be cut. Remove the top part of the box as indicated on it. Dig a hole big enough for the container and to a proper depth to provide the correct bud union height as with the other

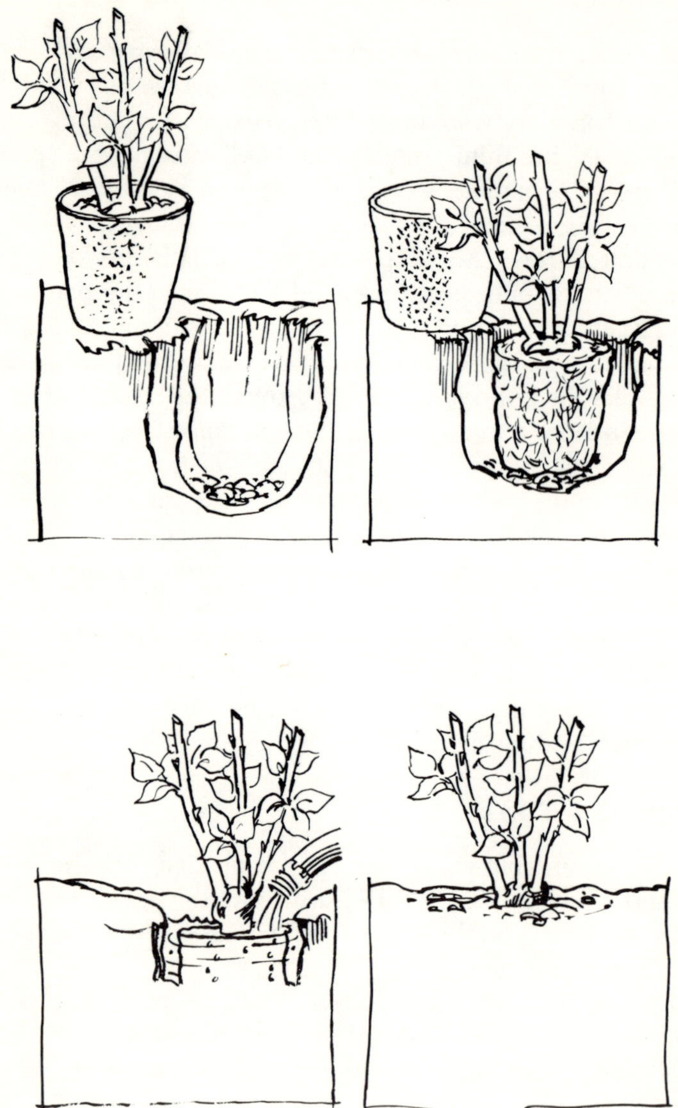

5. The four steps of planting new potted roses.

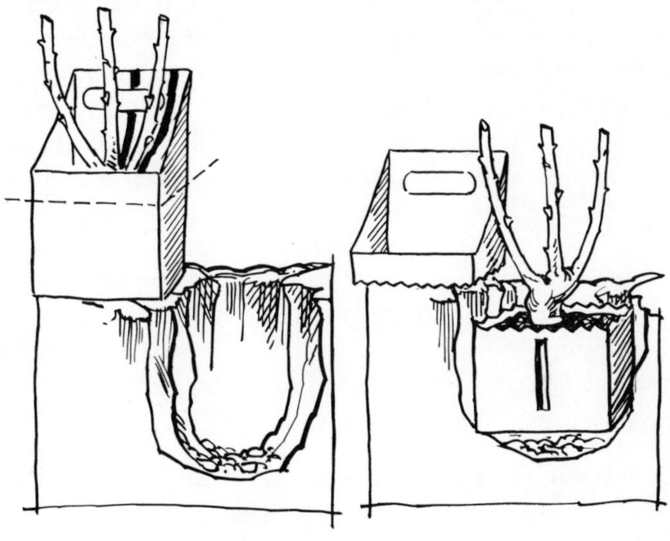

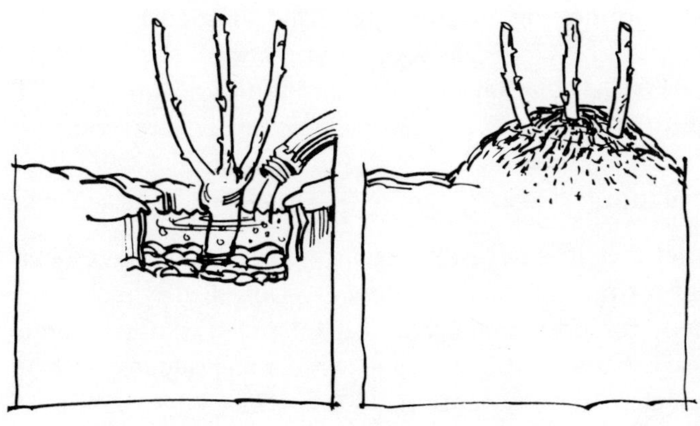

6. The four steps of planting plantable-box roses.

rose types. Cut short vertical slits into all four sides of the box. The roots will grow through the box material but these slits will allow the initial roots to get out into the surrounding soil quickly. Place the box in the hole, check the bud union height and fill the hole two-thirds full with soil. Only when this soil is in place and supporting the box, should you gently begin watering it in. Without the soil blocking the slits in the box, the media in the box will wash out, leaving no support for the plant. Finish filling the hole, bringing the soil to the original level. Water again, and make sure you have covered the box edges for a better appearance and faster decomposition of the box. If you are planting in the dormant season, mound the roses with mulch.

LAST THOUGHTS ON PLANTING ROSES

Plant Tags

All roses come with metal, plastic or paper tags wired on one of the canes to tell you what variety it is. Do not remove these tags until you have completely finished your planting as you can easily get mixed up when planting different varieties. If you snip off the tag when removing an unwanted cane, immediately wire it back on the bush. However, as soon as you are finished planting, make a map of what you have planted and remove all the tags. Tags are unsightly and give a very unprofessional look to your garden.

Transplanting Roses

Sometimes it is necessary to move roses that have been in the ground for many years to a new location. If the bush has been in one spot for over ten years, transplanting is not recommended because the rose almost never survives. The digging destroys most of the active root system.

Transplanting should only be done in the winter. You should plan on both digging and re-planting an older rose on the same day. Do not store older roses even for a short time. Cut the top two-thirds of the canes off the bush. Dig all around the plant about a foot away from the center of it, using your shovel to cut any roots you encounter. Dig progressively deeper to about 18 inches, aiming the shovel underneath the bush center as you go. Rock the loose bush back and forth, cutting the last remaining anchoring roots, and lift the bush out of the ground.

Wash off any soil on the roots and trim them, removing broken ones.

Plant the rose in the new hole as you would a new bareroot rose. Keep it well mulched. It will take the plant at least two seasons to recover from the shock of transplanting.

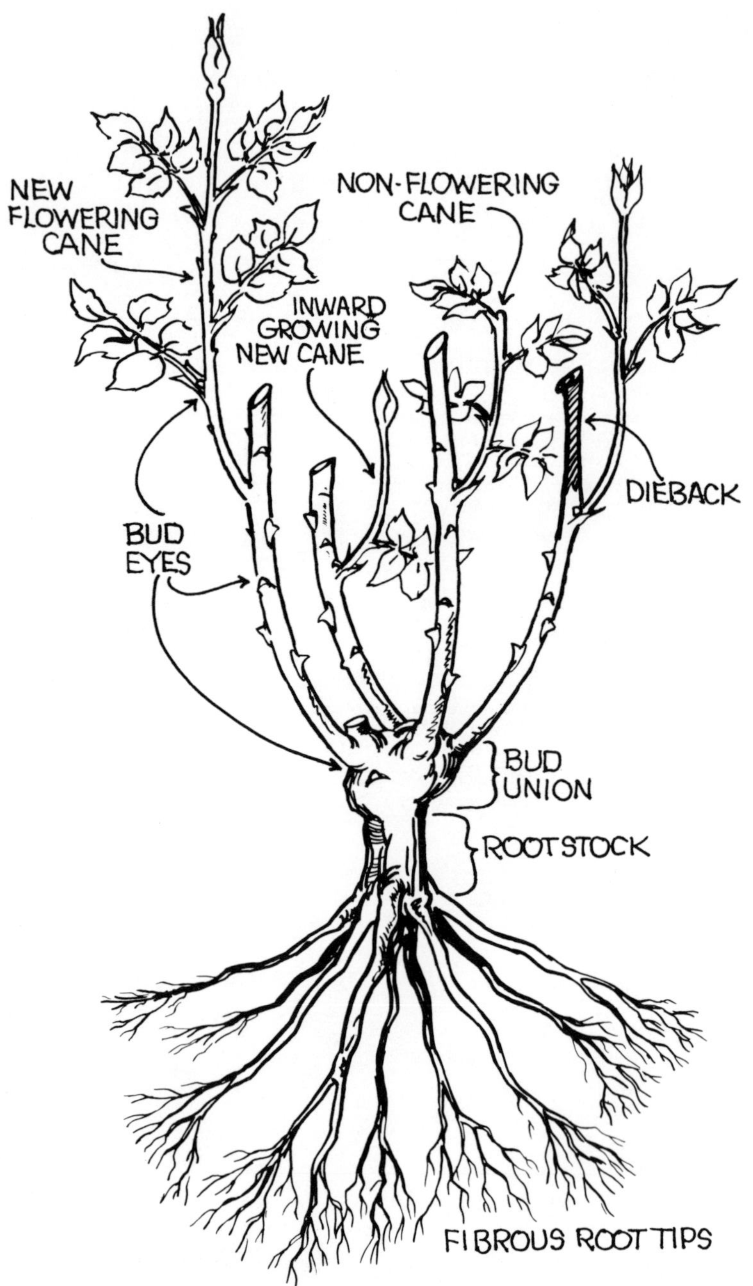

7. Anatomy of a rose in spring.

A SEASONAL APPROACH TO ROSE CARE

Roses do well in the Pacific Northwest for many reasons not the least of which is the mild seasonal variation in our weather. Roses dislike extremes of heat and cold, so our cool summers and mild winters fit their needs perfectly. It is rarely so hot in the summer that roses enter a state of semi-dormancy that stops flower formation as occurs in California. It is rarely too cold in the winter for any length of time to seriously damage existing canes and buds.

But even without extremes our seasons are different and the care you give your roses each season is also different. Luckily, there are seven tasks common to each season upon which you can base your care. These tasks will give you a feeling of continuity in your rose care.

We have defined these tasks in the following way:

Pruning: Any time you cut or remove canes, stems, flowers, and leaves from the rose bush.

Spraying: Applying a chemical in a water solution to the rose bush for the purpose of controlling or killing insect pests and diseases.

Fertilizing: Applying a nutrient to the ground to enhance the growth and health of roses.

Mulching: Applying a material to maintain the moisture in, and temperature of, the ground and to prevent weeds from growing around the rose bush.

Weeding: Removing any unwanted plants from around your rose bush.

Watering: Applying water to the rose bush.
New Roses: Any care that is needed by new plants to main-
                tain a good start.

In this chapter we present seasonal guidelines for the execution of these seven tasks. They are as simple and direct as possible to aid you in looking after your plants. Use these guidelines as a starting point in learning how to care for your roses. Don't be afraid to change or adapt these guidelines to your particular situation as your experience and confidence grows from season to season.

SPRING CARE

Working on your roses in the spring is exhilarating. It is warmer each day you are outside. The new canes and leaves, growing at a fast clip, have a bright red tinge, and are beautiful in themselves. As bright and healthy as the rose bushes look, this is the time for preventive care that will directly influence how well they will do during the stressful summer.

Pruning

Spring pruning is a delight because it is easy to work on the plant with few leaves, canes and thorns to get in the way. The main goal of your pruning now is to trim any minor damage that becomes apparent over the course of the season and to continue directing future growth for the summer. (Your major pruning should have been finished in the winter. See the Winter Section.)

The minor damage that needs to be trimmed now is called dieback. Dieback is evidenced by a brown section at the tip of an otherwise healthy green cane. This browning will usually start at the top of the cane and may spread downward killing all or part of that cane. A cane that looked strong and healthy during the winter pruning will show damage now if it has had some unseen damage from winter freezes. Dieback can also result from an insect called spring cane borers. Remove dieback by cutting into green wood below the brown portion. If an entire cane has died remove it at the bud union.

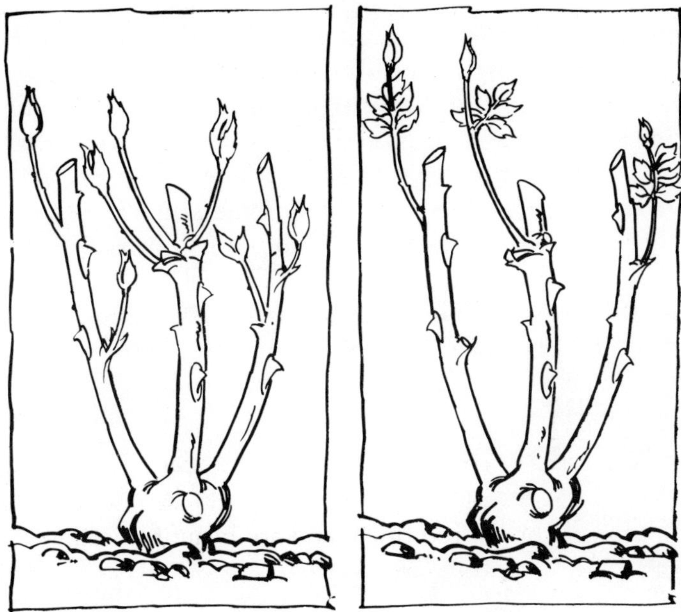

8. Remove multiple canes growing from one bud eye. Also remove inward growing canes.

If you have performed your winter pruning correctly most of the new canes will grow where you want them to grow as they expand from the bud eye. A few will not. You will see a number of new canes growing back into the center of the plant. Remove these now when they are small, by rubbing them with your finger or snipping them out. You will also see two or three thin canes expanding from one bud eye instead of one strong one. Rub or cut out the weaker canes in these groupings leaving one cane to grow from one bud eye. By removing these unwanted multiple canes early, the energy of the plant will make the remaining single cane stronger and healthier.

Spraying

Roses need protection against diseases and insects that can debilitate them and seriously affect their flower production. Like human health problems, prevention before damage is much more effective than curing the disease after the fact.

The major insect problem in the spring is aphids. Aphids, a sucking type of insect, feed on the sap of a plant by inserting their straw-like mouth part into the vein of a leaf or cane. They love cool weather and so are very troublesome both in the spring and fall. They won't defoliate a rose bush but will deform new leaves and flower buds. Another type of insect that is a problem during this season is a small green worm which chews the plant's leaves. Cane borers also do their damage in the spring on the top ends of freshly cut canes. You will see a tiny hole in the pith as evidence of the cane borer's visit. The top end of the cane will turn brown and die back.

The major fungus disease of spring is mildew, which looks like white powder on the leaf. It likes the cool, damp weather, spreads rapidly, and is more unsightly than debilitating. Black spot and rust, which like warmer temperatures, are more dangerous as they can defoliate a rose bush. You won't see these latter two problems until late spring but their invisible spores are present on the leaves and must be sprayed for now.

These insect and disease problems will attack your roses no matter where you grow them in the Pacific Northwest. You must spray before symptoms appear to prevent insect populations or diseases from building up to unmanageable levels. You should start your spray program in late March. Frequent spraying is important. Obviously, the more often you spray correctly the fewer problems you will have. Roses in open areas which have good air circulation or plant varieties which are mildew-resistant will need less spraying. A regimen of every three weeks will give you good basic protection. If you have not started early on a preventative program, start spraying as soon as problems appear.

Chemicals used to control diseases and insects change every year due to new technology or government regulation. Regardless of what a product may be called it will state on the label exactly what problem or problems it will prevent and cure. Always consult these labels to find out exactly what to use for the problems mentioned here and in the appendix.

No matter what equipment you use, spraying technique involves mixing a chemical with water and applying it to the plant in a fine mist or spray, usually under pressure. A sticker spreader (wetting agent) should be mixed with the solution to break up the water tension of the spray droplets and insure an even film of material on the leaves and canes.

You should wet both the top and underside of the leaves to the point where some of the spray drips off. The canes should also be thoroughly wet. You must spray on a dry day. If it rains heavily shortly after spraying, it would be well to spray as soon as another dry day occurs.

Safety is of paramount importance when spraying. Always wear a breathing mask, eye protection, rubber gloves, a long sleeved shirt and long pants, when handling chemicals. Wash your equipment and yourself thoroughly after you finish. Keep all chemicals and equipment locked up and out of reach of children and pets at all times.

Read all label directions thoroughly before you use a spray product. Use only the recommended doses on the label for the specific problems you have. Most fungicides and insecticides can be mixed and applied together, but the label will advise if a particular spray cannot be mixed with others. You can also obtain fungicide and insecticide combinations already mixed together. These combinations are very convenient if you have a small number of bushes.

Do not use dusts. They are more dangerous than sprays as the particle size is very fine and can be inhaled easily. They are also very unsightly on the rose leaves. Insecticide-fertilizer combinations that are spread on the ground are not very effective.

Fertilizing

More than any other phase of rose care, the subject of feeding your roses causes the greatest difference of opinion among growers. Every gardener seems to fertilize just a little bit differently and given the different types of soils, gets different results. Unlike spraying, which yields an instant response, it takes a while for the rose bush to tell you if you are feeding it correctly. In spite of all the different methods, if you provide your roses with balanced meals when they are hungry, you can't go wrong.

All roses need a variety of nutrient elements to grow well. Plant nutrients are classified as major and minor. But remember that nutrients are classified as major or minor elements only in terms of the quantity needed by the plant and not by their relative importance. Plants need minor elements just as much as they need major elements. The major elements are Nitrogen (N), Phosphorus (P), and Potassium (K). The others (Iron, Magnesium, Calcium, etc.) are lumped under the term minor or trace elements. N, P, and K have to be replaced periodically in the soil because of their heavy and continued use by the plant. N is a particular problem because it is not only leached out of the soil by rain and watering, but is heavily used by the plant as well. N must be added regularly to the soil. Although trace elements are usually present in Pacific Northwest soils, they should be added to insure an adequate supply.

The N, P, and K contents are shown on all fertilizer packages by three numbers separated by dashes. Each number, representing N, P, or K respectively, shows the percentage of element in 100 pounds of the product no matter what the size of the particular package. Thus, a 20-pound bag of 10-5-5 contains two pounds of N, one pound of P and one pound of K. Trace elements' percentage is too small to note, but a package will usually state whether they are included or not.

Fertilizers containing these major and minor elements are sold in many forms. Some are made from organic sources such as sewer sludge or animal manure. Others are synthesized from chemicals such as ammonia and phosphoric acid. Some come in a granular form which can dissolve in water, like most sack fertilizers, and some in a liquid form like fish emulsion. But no matter what form, the container must show the three major element numbers to advise you of how much of these nutrients your plants are getting. Regardless of what fertilizer you use, remember to water it in, with enough water to take it through the soil to the root zone.

The standard fertilizer to use for roses in the spring is a granular form containing about ten percent N, between five and ten percent P, between five and ten percent K and trace elements. About one-fourth cup of fertilizer should be spread evenly around the base of each rose plant a distance of 12 inches from the center in late April. Be careful not to touch the canes or leaves or bud union with the fertilizer because it will burn this tender tissue. You want your roses to use the fertilizer as soon as possible after you apply it. The plants cannot use the fertilizer unless it is in a water solution in the root zone. To ensure this, water your plants thoroughly (up to two hours with an overhead sprinkler) immediately after fertilizing.

Moderation is the key to good fertilizer application. It is easy to put on more if needed. Too much fertilizer applied at one time can lead to a serious salt build up in the soil that will burn the roots and set back your bush.

Mulching

Covering the soil surface of the rose bed with mulch does a number of very important jobs. First, mulch prevents many weed seeds from germinating. Secondly, a layer of mulch acts much like insulation in your home; it keeps the soil cooler in the summer and warmer in the winter. It also slows evaporation from the soil surface to the outside air, and so holds moisture in the soil.

Spring is the best time to apply mulch. With minimal foliage and new canes, it is easier to work around the plants without damaging them from spreading and raking the material. As with insects and diseases, prevention of weeds is more effective than cure. Applying your mulch in the spring before weed seeds form and scatter in late spring and summer will make for fewer weed problems later on.

The layer of mulch should be from one to two inches thick and cover the entire planting bed. You will have to add mulch each year, inasmuch as all mulch materials weather, reducing their bulk during the course of the year.

The material used should be weed-free. It should allow water to percolate through it, for while you want it to prevent water loss through evaporation, you don't want to impede water flow into the soil when irrigating. The Pacific Northwest is fortunate in having an abundant supply of a very excellent mulch material: barkdust. It meets all the requirements of a good mulch and is relatively inexpensive. As an added bonus barkdust is attractive when applied around roses. Well-rotted compost is another excellent mulch material. Sawdust is fine but should be a year or two old. Do not use bark chunks as this material is not effective in preventing weed growth. Black plastic is ugly and should never be used in any garden.

Weed Control

The beauty of attending to your weed problems in the spring is that as you rid your garden of existing weeds, you will be preventing new ones from starting. A weed is any unwanted plant. If left in the rose bed in any garden they rob nutrients and water from the plants you are cultivating. The spring weather makes perennial types, such as grasses, grow rapidly, as well as germinating last year's annual seeds. Most weeds, annual and perennial, will not make new seeds until the really warm temperatures of summer come, so you are not only eliminating the actual weed plants now, but many future ones as well.

Most weeds are very easily removed by hand pulling or cultivation with a hoe, trowel or shovel.

Weeds can also be killed by spraying them with herbicides. Herbicides work either by killing only the plant tissue directly contacted by the spray or by entering the plant tissue and travelling systemically throughout the leaves, stems and roots and so killing the entire plant. Most grasses can be killed with the contact type while broadleaf weeds, such as dandelion and chickweed can be killed with either the contact or systemic type, the latter doing a better job. The container label will tell both the specific herbicide type and weeds it will kill.

When spraying, wet all the visible parts of the plant

thoroughly. Do not permit spray drift on rose leaves or canes as the herbicide doesn't discriminate. So spray on a still day. The chemical must dry on the weed to be effective. The weed will usually show signs of death within one week.

Take all the safety precautions in applying herbicides you do with fungicides and insecticides. Be certain to use different equipment for herbicides and insecticides/fungicides. An herbicide spray tank used for insect spray, even though washed thoroughly, may contain an herbicide residue that will harm the roses.

No matter what method you use, hand or chemical, plan on checking your rose beds for weeds every two weeks beginning in early March.

New Roses

You have to pamper your new roses during their first season. A few simple chores performed in the spring will reward you with both good growth and flowers.

Remove the mounding material around the beginning of May. Be careful not to break off any new canes. These canes will be yellow due to the mulch cover, but they will green up rapidly when exposed to the sunshine. You may discover some dieback. Prune this out as with older roses. Do not fertilize now, as the new plants have plenty of nutrient reserves for their initial growth and fertilizer applied now may burn the new tender root tips. Lastly, watch for any sign of moisture stress, such as wilting or a very slow rate of growth. You may have to water the new roses if the spring is particularly warm and little rain has fallen.

SUMMER

Roses are beautiful in the summer. Heat and sunshine make them thrive. You are out of doors a great deal of the time now to enjoy them, so it isn't very hard to give them the care that will maintain their spring start.

Pruning

The objectives of summer pruning are to keep your rose bushes constantly producing flowers and new canes, as well as maintaining healthy growth.

The process of forming flowers on a rose plant is simple. A bud eye from an existing cane (those remaining from your winter pruning) expands and grows during the spring into a new cane. The new cane forms leaves and new bud eyes at the junction of the new leaves and stem. When the new cane has matured to its final length it forms flower buds which expand into flowers. The flowers bloom, fade and form seeds encapsulated in hips, the fruit of the rose plant. So far the plant has done this all on its own.

If the developing seed hips are permitted to grow you will have few if any flowers from the bush for the rest of the season. The seeds produce a hormone which travels back down the canes inhibiting the cane's bud eyes from expanding and growing into *new* flowering canes. If you remove the old bloom and attending seed hip, the flowering process will start over again at other bud eyes. The bud eyes below your cut will receive no hormone to inhibit them and so will grow into new flowering canes. This simple act of cutting the faded flowers is the whole secret to keeping your plants flowering. It needs to be repeated on all your plants, all summer, to keep your roses in continual bloom until frost.

There is no great mystery about the best way to cut old blooms. As always look at your plant. Forget everything and anything you have ever read or been told about cutting the stem to a five leaflet leaf. The main considerations affecting where and how you should cut when removing old blooms are whether your plant is a tall, short or medium high bush, with an individual flower on a long stem or clusters of flowers at the end of the canes.

If your plant is a tall grower (Peace is a good example) with new canes growing two to three feet tall (from where they sprouted from the existing cane to the top of their flowers) don't be afraid to remove most of this cane when you cut. The bud eye, which should be an inch or less below your cut, will expand out of the lower section of the cane and produce a new flowering cane in four to six weeks. It will grow to about the same height as the first cane. If you are afraid of removing too much growth and cut only a little below the faded flower, the bud eye below this cut will expand into a thin cane with few flowers. These latter flowers will be small and subject to wind and rain damage.

On a medium or short growth-habit plant (such as the floribunda Cathedral) new canes will only grow one to two feet from where they started. Cut out correspondingly lesser amounts of cane below the faded flowers. No matter what the growth habit of the bush remember that new good canes can only come from the lower, thick section of the previous flowering cane.

The other consideration is the number of flowers growing at the end of the flowering cane regardless of rose classification. Whether a hybrid tea, grandiflora, floribunda, or climber, if there is one flower on the end of a cane, prune the cane as soon as the color fades or the petals drop off. If there are two or more flowers at the end of the cane you will notice that they open and fade individually over a period of time. You have a choice as to how to remove these multi-flowered clusters. If you have the time you can snip out individual flowers as they fade, not disturbing the unopened flowers. The other option, and by far easier, is to wait until all the flowers in the cluster have faded. In either case, when the last flower in the cluster has faded you can cut the canes below the branching cluster growth according to the above growth habit guidelines. Waiting until all the flowers have faded before cutting is especially recommended for small flowered floribundas with up to two dozen flowers in a cluster.

Plan on checking your plants every two weeks until mid-September for faded blooms. Any flowers that fail to open for whatever reason should also be pruned. By cutting these old blooms, not only will you have more flowers but your bushes will look neater.

Cut out any dieback which continues to appear in the summer. It will be difficult to see inasmuch as the foliage obscures the inner areas of the plant, but by careful examining each plant you can spot it.

9. The main considerations affecting where you should cut when removing old bloom are the size of the bush and the type of flower growth.

During the summer, light green canes will occasionally emerge from the ground below the bud union. The leaves of these canes are light green, delicate and do not look at all like the existing leaves of the plant. These canes are called understock or suckers and are an attempt by the rootstock (which is a different species from the grafted plant) to bypass the bud union and make canes of its own. They are unsightly and useless. Remove them by cutting them out as far down into the ground as possible. Tree roses may develop suckers on the exposed trunk. Cut these suckers flush with the trunk, being careful not to cut into the trunk.

A word of caution. Do not confuse the unwanted understock with the wanted new flowering canes coming from a bud eye on the bud union. Flowering canes are thick and reddish and have leaves of the same size and texture as the existing leaves, so you can easily distinguish them from understock. These bud union canes—called basal breaks—will appear all summer. Basal breaks are a sign of a healthy plant. The more basal breaks you have the more canes you will have to choose from in your winter pruning, allowing you to retire older canes which produce fewer flowers.

10. If you look carefully you can easily tell the difference between wanted basal breaks and unwanted suckers.

A special note about climbers. Climbers produce new canes from the bud union which are usually long and floppy and get in the way. Tie these new canes loosely on your trellis just to get them out of the way and prevent breakage. You will need them in the fall when you prune.

Spraying

Summer insect and disease control is a matter of continuing a good spring program, while adjusting it for special summer pests and application problems.

Black spot and rust will show up now, as both fungi thrive in summer heat. Spider mites are a heat-loving pest which inhabit the underside of the leaf and will appear during this season. These three problems are extremely serious because unlike aphids or mildew, black spot, rust and spider mites can defoliate a plant in a short time. Since the leaves produce food upon which all new growth and flowers depend, you can quickly be left with a stunted, flowerless rose bush. You should be spraying now with chemicals that specifically state they will alleviate these problems.

Thrips, tiny black insects that inhabit the flower petals, also thrive in summer heat but do little flower damage to a healthy plant. Insecticides that control aphids and mites will usually control thrips also, but again check the label.

Summer spraying techniques are somewhat special. Never spray on a very hot day. When the temperature is above 85 degrees F. the spray solution dries out rapidly on the leaves leaving a chemical deposit that may burn young foliage. Always spray *after* you water, so that you do not wash off the chemical.

As pests may build up immunities to specific sprays, change spray materials occasionally (as long as each specific product states on the label that it will kill or prevent the problem you have). If you are not getting good results with a specific product never increase the recommended dosage. Instead, increase the frequency of application, within the limits recommended on the label. If you continue to have poor results switch to another product.

If you have been faithful in your spring prevention spraying you will find your summer problems much less serious than those who start spraying when the summer diseases first appear. The summer schedule should be stopped about September 10. By this time most diseases and insects are transforming themselves into their over-wintering stages, on which summer spray products have little effect. Furthermore, heavy fall rains make it almost impossible to find a decent day on which to spray.

Fertilizing

Summer is when the rose bush will tell you if you have been feeding it well. If the leaves are large, leathery and deep green, if new buds break and grow rapidly into canes of large diameter, and if you are getting plenty of flowers with clear strong colors, you are probably doing a good job of feeding your plants.

Feeding in the summer must be timed according to the flushes of flower growth. Even though roses produce flowers all season long, there are identifiable periods when there are more flowers in bloom on the plant than at other times. Depending on weather and local conditions, these peak blooming periods usually occur in June, late July to early August, and in September. As explained in the summer pruning section, remove the old bloom during and after these peak periods. New canes will immediately start to grow below your cuts. This is when the rose bush needs another meal. You should plan on giving each plant about one-fourth cup of a granular fertilizer in late June and early August. Do not fertilize past August 31 as a late summer application promotes too much tender growth in the fall which may be damaged in an early frost.

While the amount of fertilizer given in each summer application is the same as in the spring the percentage of the nutrient elements is different. As mentioned before nitrogen must be supplied constantly while the supply of phosphorous and potassium in the spring application is usually adequate for the whole season. Fertilizer applied in the summer should contain about ten percent N

with low concentrations of between one and five percent of both
P and K.

Watering

Roses are very heavy drinkers during the warm months. Keeping their thirst satisfied is an important summer maintenance chore. Water is absolutely necessary for a plant which will produce flowers, be vigorous and resist insects and diseases. The delicate petals of the flowers need a constant supply of water to open and expand fully. Fertilizer can only be taken up by the plant in a water solution. Soil micro-organisms and worms (both important for good soil structure) work best in a moist soil. Without adequate water, leaves will turn papery and take on a gray-green color as compared to the leathery texture and deep green of a leaf containing adequate water.

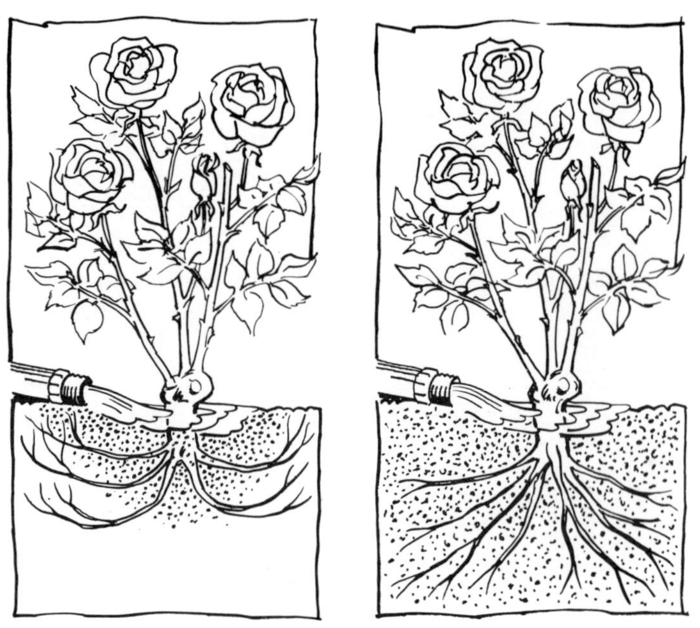

11. Water deeply to promote deep fibrous roots.

In order to assure that the plant has an adequate water supply, you must water for a long time at each application. Four hours or more of irrigation at each watering will allow the water to percolate deeply into the soil. Deep penetration of water increases the soil volume that the roots can depend on for water. It encourages the roots to grow deeply into the soil where it is cool and moist. If you water the roses for brief periods (less than four hours) only the top layer of soil is thoroughly wet which in turn encourages the roots to grow only near the soil surface. This vulnerable area dries out very quickly when the weather is hot damaging the root tips and subjecting the plant to stress, which in turn slows growth and flower production.

Roses should be watered frequently as well as deeply. They should be watered every two weeks starting June 1st assuming our usual dry summers. However, during periods of heavy summer rains or temperatures below 65 degrees F. you need water less frequently. When we have several days of strong, dry, east winds or temperatures above 85 degrees F., you must water weekly. You should maintain your watering schedule until September 15.

No matter what the weather, sandy soils will dry out more rapidly than clay soils, and so require more frequent watering.

There are many different ways to water, all of which are fine as long as you keep long duration and frequency in mind. You can water anytime during the day or night. It also doesn't matter whether you water from over the rose bushes or from ground level. While it is true overhead watering may spread some diseases, a single summer downpour may spread the same amount of disease. Overhead watering has two beneficial effects. It washes the dust and pollutants off the leaves. It also helps to keep spider mites under control, as mites like dusty, dry surfaces and decline in numbers after a good watering.

New Roses

New roses should, if you bought good healthy plants and took care in establishing them, produce flowers for you during the first summer. As with older bushes the flower should be cut off after they have faded. Flowers on new rose bushes will not have stems as long as established roses of the same variety and, therefore, should be treated as short or medium habit plants when removing the old bloom.

Start fertilizing in late June at the same time as your second application on your older plants. Use one-fourth cup of ten percent N, five to ten percent P and five to ten percent K formulation. Fertilize again in early August with the same fertilizer you apply to your older bushes. Water the fertilizer in well on both occasions.

Keep a very close watch on your watering. A deep soaking once a week is not too much for new roses since it is critical to give them a good first season's growth by encouraging the small root system to quickly grow as deep as possible.

FALL

Your roses are particularly special in the fall. All their efforts are directed to giving you those last beautiful flowers before winter. Somehow the colors seem brighter when contrasted against cloudy days and early sunsets.

Pruning

Fall pruning is the easiest rose pruning to do. In many ways it is very satisfying, as the feeling of completing the growing season is never more apparent than at this time. There is also the possibility now that you might find that last unspoiled rose to bring into the house.

Fall pruning can be done anytime from November until mid-December. It consists of cutting away the top part of the rose bush and removing all the leaves. By removing the top heavy one-third of the bush the plant presents much less resistance to winter winds that may loosen the root system in the ground. With the leaves gone, there are fewer places for disease spores and insects to over-winter.

Cut the bush down about one-third or to waist height, whichever is lower. Determine the height for each plant and simply cut all the canes straight across at that level.

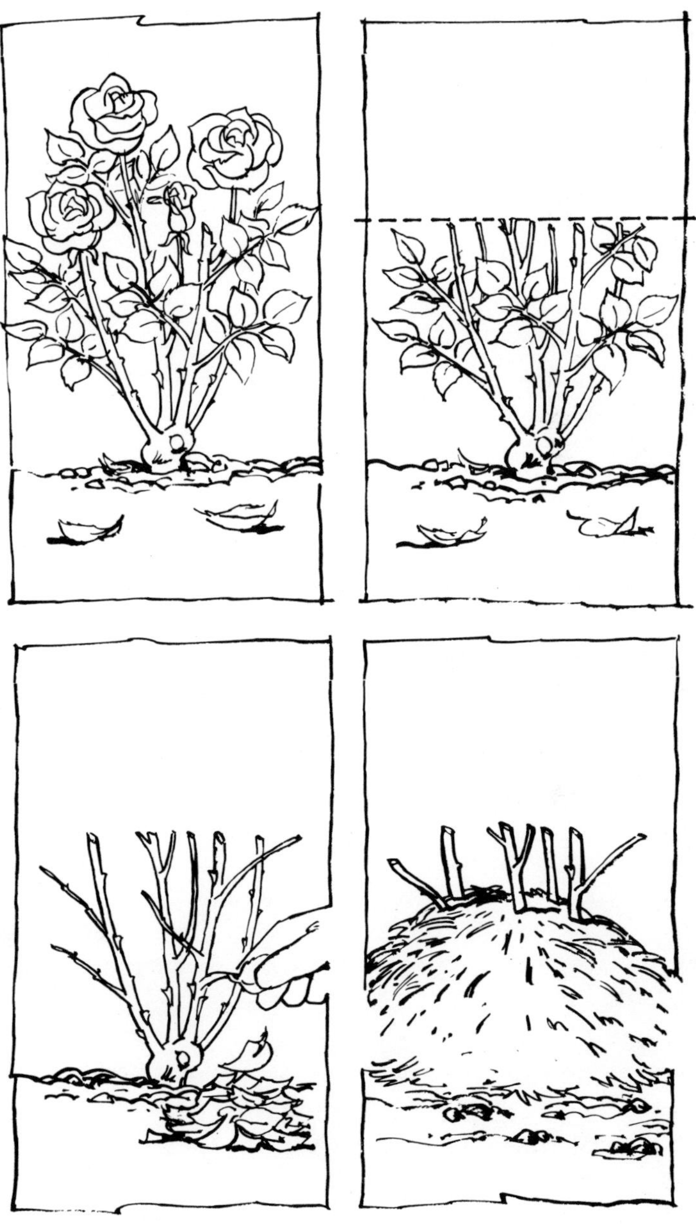

12. Preparation for winter includes topping, leaf-stripping and mounding.

Next strip off all the leaves remaining on the canes. Grasp the petiole (leaf stalk) with a gloved hand and pull the leaf sharply downward. The leaf is only loosely attached at this time of the year as the plant responds to lower temperatures. Discard or burn all canes and leaves. Do *not* compost them or use them as mulch. Most disease spores will survive the composting process.

Climbers should be treated differently. They should be heavily pruned and trained now. There are three steps to pruning climbers for successful flowering next season. First you must remove all the canes from the framework supporting them by removing whatever ties you used to attach the canes to the framework. The second step is to prune out very old wood and very weak wood. The third step is to retie the remaining canes to your support in a way to give you the maximum number of flowers next year.

As always, look at your climber before you start to get an idea of how it grew this past season and how you want it to grow next season. Then, cut all the ties from the previous year so all the canes are free of the framework which supported them. Also remove any ties you used temporarily to keep the new summer canes from breaking.

Secondly, remove as much older wood as possible while leaving a sufficient number of canes to work with later. Depending on the variety you should have four to eight canes of varying length remaining. The older wood is conspicuous by its barky, spiny, gray-brown appearance and thick diameter. They should be cut out close to the bud union. Also remove any very thin or very short canes (relative to the average cane diameter and length of the particular variety). Strip all the leaves off the remaining canes.

The third step, training, is performed now because the long canes are still flexible and won't break when bent.

Climbers will have more flowers on canes that are bent horizontally than canes that are tied or left to grow vertically. By bending the long canes you force the bud eyes all along the cane to break into short canes or stems with flower clusters at the end of them next summer. Canes that grow straight up only grow these short flowering canes at their tips. Take this fact into account before re-tying the canes on your support. Use your imagination and tie any way you wish (fan shapes or curlicues are popular) but try to train them horizontally or curved back toward the ground if possible. Be careful not to break the canes as you bend them. You will see the difference in flower production in the coming season.

Tie all canes to your support with twine using a double knot. The knot should be tight enough to hold the cane to the support but should not cut into the cane. Make lots of ties. The canes will become very heavy with summer blooms and foliage and what seems like plenty of support now won't be enough in the growing season.

Mulching

After you have topped and stripped the leaves off the roses you should mound up your roses for the winter. Mounding protects the bud union and canes from serious freeze damage.

Any loose material such as bark dust is excellent for this purpose. An added advantage to bark dust is that when you remove the mound in the spring you can use this same bark dust as a spring mulch on the rose bed.

The mound should be about one foot high and completely cover the bud union and lower part of the canes.

Weed Control

Fall rains and cooler temperatures produce perfect conditions for seed germination and you will find many weeds in your rose beds now. Weedkillers are less effective in the cool weather than in the summer so you will have to remove most of these weeds by hand. Combined with leaf stripping, weeding leaves the rose beds neat, tidy and clean and, hence, a pleasure to look at during the winter.

New Roses

By now, the new roses you have planted during the past year are well established and can be cared for in the same way as your established plants.

But, what about next year? You probably have some roses that are very old, have performed poorly or, most importantly, that you just don't like. You've also seen some new varieties at a public garden or in a friend's garden that looked interesting. Finally, the rose catalogs are starting to arrive with their enticing pictures and descriptions.

Now is the time to plan your new roses for next season. First decide on what will be removed and/or what new areas will have to be prepared. Prepare the ground now so everything will be ready when the new roses arrive. Plan your spacing so you'll know how many plants you'll need. Finally, if using a mail order nursery, place your order as soon as you have decided what you want. No matter when the roses are sent out to you, requests are filled in the order in which they are received. So early ordering ensures that you will get new and popular varieties which are always in short supply.

WINTER

It is cold and wet and hard to think of doing anything in the garden now. Think of summer instead and of the beautiful roses you had last year and those yet to come. Put on something warm and waterproof and go out into the garden to do what needs to be done. There isn't much, but it is of great importance.

Pruning

Winter pruning is that great subject that most of you face with apprehension. Somehow, watering, fertilizing and pest control can all be worked out and understood. But, oh, pruning! Well don't despair, it is impossible to kill a rose bush by improper pruning. Furthermore, by following the guidelines below, you can't help but do it properly.

Winter pruning has only one purpose: it is to leave only strong healthy canes that will produce the best summer flowers. If you keep this in mind, you can't go wrong. This purpose is achieved by eliminating weak and dead growth; by opening the center of the bush for better light penetration and air circulation; by directing future growth away from the center; and by lowering all the canes to their thicker lower sections so the new growth will be strong, straight and tall. Ideally, after you prune you will have a bush with five to seven canes radiating out from the center.

Here is how you go about it. Remove your mounding material and study the plant for a moment. Walk around the bush and look at it from all sides. Get a feel for how you want it to grow in the coming season. Look at the canes. Get an idea of their relative thickness, height and angle of growth. Now you are ready to bring pruning shears to the canes.

Always start with the obvious and then go to the discretionary. There should be some obvious canes to cut out first. Remove any dead, shrivelled or broken canes. Remove very skinny or weak wood. All your preliminary cuts should be made flush with the bud union or whatever good wood the unwanted cane is growing from. On hybrid teas and grandifloras remove canes that are less than pencil thickness. On floribundas, thin wood is relative to the average thickness of the canes. Remove any canes that are extremely old, providing there are enough good young ones to work with later. The surface of these old canes will be spiny and corky and they will be brown or gray colored. These older canes are usually growing directly from the bud union. On some rose, however, good canes grow out of old canes a few inches above the bud union. In this case you leave the older wood because if you remove it, you remove the good newer canes also. You should, when through, have a number of smooth, green canes of varying height.

At this point you have removed all the obvious expendable wood, now comes the hard part—deciding which canes will provide the best growth for the coming season.

You want to open up the center of the plant and direct future growth outward. Remove one cane of any two which are crossing, leaving either the stronger of the two, or the cane that grows away from the center. Cut out one of any two canes that are growing very close together and look like they will interfere with each other. Lastly reduce the height of all the canes to 18 to 24 inches for hybrid teas and grandifloras, and 12 to 18 inches for floribundas.

The final cut on each remaining cane should be a slanting one about one-fourth inch above an outward facing bud eye. The bud eyes directly below the cuts will break first and grow the best in the spring. For the same reasons that the remaining canes should face outward, the bud eyes should face outward too. If the canes are cut with the bud eyes facing inward, they will expand and grow back into the center of the plant where they will compete with each other for light and air. By growing away from the center each cane and flower will grow to its maximum potential.

Lastly, paint your cuts with any good tree pruning compound to prevent cane borer damage in the spring.

As mentioned, the resulting ideal is a bush of five to seven strong green canes radiating outward from the center of the bush. The resulting reality is usually different particularly if you are

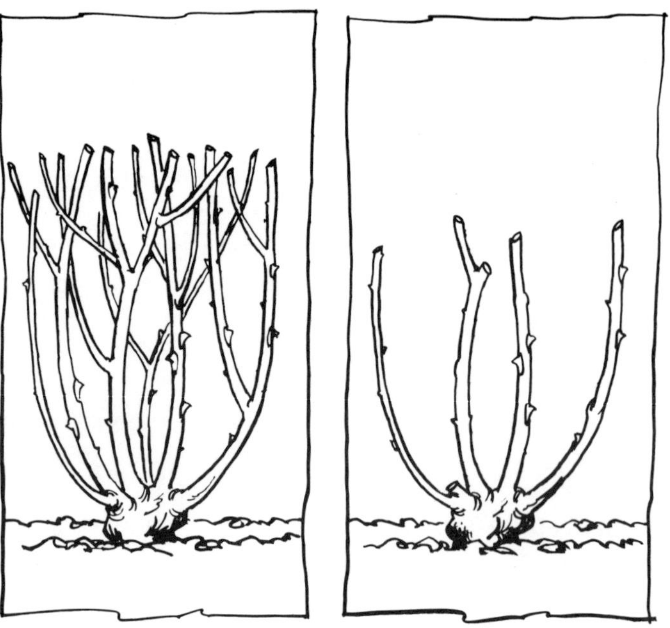

13. Winter pruning—the end result is an uncluttered plant ready to grow in the spring.

working with very new or very old plants or plants that haven't been properly cared for. After doing all the required pruning you may end up with only one or two decent canes. You are probably afraid that you cut out too much wood. Don't worry, as good flowers only come from a strong existing cane. Weak canes produce weak shoots and only a few small flowers. Better to have a few good canes using the energy of the plant efficiently than many weak ones producing nothing. Furthermore, by cutting out the weak wood, you will encourage new growth from the bud union next spring.

Late February to early March is the best time to prune in the Pacific Northwest. The worst of the cold weather is past and the plants are preparing for spring growth. Don't prune on a freezing day as the canes may be brittle and break easily. Also, don't worry about trying to save any bud eyes that might have expanded already because of warm February weather. The bud eyes below your new cuts will expand into new canes once you have finished pruning.

Occasionally, the Pacific Northwest suffers a very cold winter with extended periods of freezing temperatures (below 20 degrees F) that may damage the rose canes no matter how well you have mounded them. This damage will evidence itself when you make your pruning cuts as brown pith in the center of what appears to be a perfectly good green cane. No matter how green these canes look on the outside they will die back in the spring when the temperature rises.

If you spot a cane showing brown pith while doing your regular winter pruning, remove it. Cut short sections of cane off until you see healthy white pith. If the whole cane contains brown pith, cut it out flush with the bud union.

The above pruning techniques will work better if you use the right tools. The three important tools for pruning are hand pruning shears, a pair of long-handled lopping shears and a small folding saw. Scissor-type shears (secateurs), both hand and loppers, are preferred over the "blade and anvil" type because they are easier on your hands and leave a clean cut. Never try to cut a cane that is too big for the tool. If the cane won't cut easily with the hand shears, try the loppers. If the lopper won't cut it easily, use the saw. By using the right size tool you avoid twisting and so damaging the shears. With the correct tool you always end up with a clean cut at the end of the cane instead of a ragged one which is sloppy looking and promotes disease.

Spraying

Insect and disease pests are not actively damaging your plants during the winter. Still, they are present in a perhaps more insidious form—the over-wintering stage. Be they fungus spores or hard encapsulations of insects, over-wintering stages are built to withstand the rigors of winter. These protective devices also withstand ordinary summer spray products and, therefore, stronger ones are needed. Luckily, roses are also dormant in winter and the stronger chemicals won't hurt them. Spraying now will greatly reduce the number of pests that will bother your roses next spring and summer.

You should use two products now. The fungicide material may be a combination of chemicals but it will always say "dormant spray" somewhere on the label. The insecticide is miscible oil. Sprayed on the roses it will coat any dormant insects and suffocate them. As with summer chemicals, mix these dormant season sprays exactly as recommended on their labels and observe all safety precautions.

Spray the chemicals on the roses, completely wetting all canes and the surrounding ground. You must spray on a dry day for greatest effect. In fact, a couple of dry days after your application should be hoped for, although seldom realized during our winters. Spray at least twice each winter leaving a couple of weeks between applications. Your last application of dormant spray should be done immediately after winter pruning. Never use dormant spray products past mid-March. Dormant sprays are strong chemicals and may burn the tips of newly expanding canes.

Fertilizing

You don't fertilize your roses in the winter but you can test the soil to give you an exact picture of what your plants may need next season in the way of nutrients.

If you used the general fertilizer guidelines outlined for spring and summer, your roses probably did well. But you may have a special soil situation or are so excited about your roses that you want to be more exact in you future care. If either is the case, testing your soil is the tool needed to provide the answer.

The best way to test your soil is to send it to a state soil laboratory. First write them for the necessary forms, fee schedule and sampling instructions (see address in appendix). Follow the directions and send the sample to the lab. There, they will run a series of chemical tests on your soil and make recommendations for you based on the test results.

There will be a lot of numbers on your soil test report that you receive back from the lab. Don't be confused. The important items are the soil pH reading and the amount of Potassium (P) and Phosphorous (K) present (N is rarely tested due to its leachability).

The pH, to a large extent, controls nutrient availability in the soil. If the soil is too acid or too alkaline, the plant is unable to take up the needed elements. The pH should read between 6.1 and 6.8. If it is lower than this range, an application rate for lime to bring pH to the desired level will be included.

The parts per million (ppm) of P and K should read about 100 and 300 respectively. If these numbers are too high, you have an excess amount of fertilizer salts in the soil which is not good for the plants. The soil lab will usually recommend using a fertilizer which has little or no P and K (such as ammonium sulphate, 15-0-0), for one or two seasons until your soil test results show P and K at an acceptable level.

MINIATURE ROSES

Whether doll houses or model trains, small things appeal to all of us because of their charm and delicacy. They also have the ability to overshadow, by subtle understatement, that which is bigger and brighter. Miniature roses share these characteristics of all small things. They also are practical and easy to care for.

LANDSCAPING WITH MINIATURES

It is hard to resist the wide variety of miniature roses. The delicate leaves and flowers are similar to their bigger cousins in everything but size. They bloom profusely. Their color range is enormous. Incredible as it may seem, with miniatures you can have an entire rose garden in a planter box.

Miniature roses (popularly called minis) grow about one foot tall. They have miniature foliage in proportion to the flowers. The range of flower forms include single, open type flowers as well as the high centered double, hybrid tea type. There are even miniature tree roses and miniature climbers that can be trained on a small trellis or used in hanging baskets. Like bigger roses, they also have to be placed in the garden with thought as to how they will be most effective.

Charming as they are, minis must be framed in the garden. They can be lost in a landscape view or among other plants if not set off by a frame. Fortunately, it is easy to highlight them. The most effective way to do this is to raise the plants above ground level; one foot or more above the surrounding area immediately sets them off, while bringing the roses closer to eye level. Another way to frame them is to separate them from other plants. The best way to do this is to grow them in a container or planter box, or you can highlight minis by having a planting follow an existing landscape line such as a deck rail or walkway.

The most effective and enjoyable way to use minis which incorporates all of the previous landscaping suggestions is to grow miniature roses in containers. Ceramic pots, redwood tubs, barrel halves, window boxes, even plastic pots can be used. Containers can be used in small spaces like apartment balconies, decks and patios. They are great grouped together or singly in a spot which is too small for anything else. Minis are subtle. They don't overpower you, and when they are grown in pots they are in proportion to their surroundings. In addition, if you have a large container garden, you can also plant some low growing floribundas in pots too. Floribundas' slightly larger size—bush, leaves and flower—will add a little variety to any group of potted minis without overshadowing them.

BUYING MINIATURES

Miniature roses are grown commercially from rooted cuttings and are sold in small pots. Since they are pot grown, they are available year around and are easy to plant. They can be purchased either from a local garden center or mail order nursery. Always check the foliage and canes for any damage at the garden center or upon receiving them in the mail from a nursery. Damp soil in the pot and a healthy green color on the tiny canes are signs of a good plant.

PLANTING MINIATURES

Miniature roses like sun and well-drained soil in their permanent home. Their extensive fibrous root system needs good soil to thrive. If you plant the roses in the ground, amend the soil with organic matter to promote drainage and the growth of soil organisms. The pH level should be between 6.1 and 6.8. Add lime if the pH is lower. If you plan to plant them in a raised bed amend both the soil that you add and the underlying four to six inches of the existing soil.

If you are going to grow minis in containers, a commercially prepared potting mix is excellent. You can also make your own potting mix with equal parts of peat moss, sand or vermiculite, and good garden soil.

Before you plant make sure the rose is damp. Dig your hole with a trowel a little bit larger than the pot. Knock the plant out of the pot and plant it so that it is about one-quarter inch deeper than it was in the pot. Since these are rooted cuttings there is no bud union height to be concerned about. *Lightly* firm the soil around the plant and water it in well. Apply a light mulch, one-half to three-fourths inch, of fine bark and watch it grow. You can plant any time of the year as long as the ground isn't frozen and air temperature is above 40 degrees F.

Your minis can be transplanted, too. You may be a gardener who likes to change things evey few years or just wants to give a friend a plant that has done particularly well for you. Lift your miniature rose by digging straight down in a circle about 3-4 inches from the center of the plant and about 6 inches deep with your shovel. Aim the shovel in toward and underneath the center of the rose. When you have dug all the way around the plant, you can lift it out of the ground with your shovel. Plant the bush in your new spot immediately and water it in well (same procedure as for new miniature roses). Old miniatures may have formed both a very dense crown and root system so you can divide the plant in half with your pruning shears or sharp shovel and get two plants if you desire. Both divisions will do well if planted as soon as possible. Don't try dividing plants only a few years old.

SEASONAL CARE

The type of care you give your minis is similar to larger roses, but again on a smaller scale.

Pruning

The primary pruning objective is to keep them from becoming crowded and twiggy. Both of these conditions promote fungus disease and spider mite infestations. (Flower production and flower size don't vary greatly with heavy or light pruning.) Prune them in late February or early March. Concentrate on removing extremely thin wood and broken or dead canes leaving a lot of good canes. You don't need to cut to outward facing buds or prune to an exact height; anywhere between three and six inches high is fine. In fact, you can even give them a butch cut at any height between three and six inches and let it go at that.

During the summer, plan on snipping out the faded flowers (don't remove too much stem), mainly to provide the plant with air circulation and to keep the plant looking neat. Miniatures don't set much seed so there are few hormones to inhibit successsive blooms. Your minis will continue to flower even if you don't regularly get around to cutting the old blooms.

Spraying

The worst mini pest is spider mites. These tiny insects' idea of paradise is to be on the underside of a miniature rose leaf; the dense growth habit and low position provide perfect conditions for mite infestation. They can defoliate the rose plant rapidly. To eliminate this pest you must not only spray with a product that specifically states that it will kill mites, but also adjust your spraying technique so that you thoroughly cover the underside of the leaves. By directing your spray from below you will not only put the chemical where it is needed to control present and future insect generations, but also physically wash away some of the existing mites. In fact, washing your minis with a medium-strength stream of water every two weeks (before you spray any fungicide or insecticide) will help keep the mite problem within bounds. You will find spraying much easier if your roses are higher than ground level, either in a raised bed or container.

Fertilizing

Moderation is the key to feeding miniatures. Large amounts of fertilizer just encourages some canes to grow thick and tall—up to one foot—above the average height of the plant which destroys the miniature effect. Use fertilizers with five percent or less of Nitrogen (N), five percent or less of Phosphorus (P), and five percent or less of Potassium (K), at each application. Apply only about a teaspoon of a granular type per plant. Miniatures' bursts of growth are not as pronounced as the flushes of larger bushes so a once-a-month application from May until August is perfect. Of course, the bushes must be watered well immediately after fertilizing.

Lastly, while dry granular fertilizers are all right, you will probably get better results with a liquid fertilizer, either organic or chemical. The tightly packed fibrous root systems of the minis seem to respond better to these liquid type fertilizers. Apply about a cup, diluted according to the product recommmendations, per plant every month from May until August.

Watering

Miniature rose roots don't grow deeply into the soil. They are very fibrous with a mass of delicate root hairs. For these reasons, you must be even more attentive to irrigation than with the larger roses. Once a week from June until late September, would not be too much even when the weather is cool. You must water more often if the weather is above 85 degrees F.

Minis in containers, like all potted plants, are very sensitive to hot weather. Their water reserves are limited to that contained in the pot—an amount that can be drained dry by leaf transpiration in one hot day. Check your potted plants often and if the soil surface is dry or the leaves look papery, water them. A well-watered, healthy plant will reward you with an abundance of deep green leaves, new growing canes, and a multitude of flowers.

Mulching

The mulch around minis should never exceed one inch and one-half inch is really better. Barkdust or rotted compost is best. The mulch will keep the soil moist and cool as well as minimizing problems with weeds.

Never use any chemical herbicide close to minatures. It is impossible even on a very still day to prevent the spray from drifting onto the miniature rose foliage and doing extensive damage. You must weed by hand with either a small hoe or trowel. Check your plants for emerging weeds frequently. Once weeds like morning glory, dandelion or quackgrass are established in a miniature rose bed or pot and entwined with the rose roots, it is impossible to eliminate them short of digging up some or all of your plants.

Minis are surprisingly hardy plants for their demure stature. When planted in the ground a one-half to one-inch covering of mulch will protect them enough from the worst of our Pacific Northwest winters. Only if you are in a very cold or frosty area or are subject to strong east winds in the winter should you add another inch of mulch during the winter months.

Container plants must be additionally protected. Their roots, more prone to freeze damage than the canes, are separated from the cold by only the thickness of the pot itself. Bring your pots into an unheated garage or basement so they stay dormant for the winter. Another way to protect them is to store the containers alongside a fence or side of a house and then cover the containers with barkdust. The mulch adds additional inches between the root zone and the cold. Water the plants before you store them so they don't dry out during the winter.

MINIATURES AS HOUSE PLANTS

Your minis are growing well outside and you are thinking that it might be nice to have roses blooming by a window in January. They seem to be the right size to grow indoors, but are they good house plants?

Most house plants are tropical shade-loving or shade-tolerant species that adapt well to warm, low-humidity, low-light, winter house conditions. Minis are outdoor, hardy, temperate-zone plants that require a lot of light and air circulation. The conditions required by minis are simply lacking in the home during the winter. Without adequate light you won't have many flowers or a healthy plant. Without good air circulation, your insect and disease problems will explode to unmanageable proportions and infect all your other houseplants. Furthermore, like all roses, minis need a period of dormancy every year during the cold months to rest. They simply cannot sustain a year-round growth cycle. They will impose dormancy on themselves if you don't give it to them, leading to their death in a hot, dry, indoor situation.

You can, however, have moderate success if you treat your minis as a one-season plant and don't try to grow them in the house from year to year.

If you decide to try minis indoors, buy new, fresh plants in September or October. Never bring in plants that you have been growing outside all summer. Pot the new plants in a good houseplant soil mix. Place them in the sunniest window (minimum six hours of direct light) that you have. A west or south facing exposure is best. Fertilize the plants with a liquid solution once a month as long as they are actively growing. Spray for insects and disease at least every three weeks. Take your minis either outdoors or to a well-ventilated spot to spray them, and make sure they are dry before they are returned to their original location. Don't spray them where they are displayed as the spray residue will linger in the air for unprotected people to breathe.

Keep the air humid with a humidifier or pebble tray with water underneath the pots. Finally, remove your plants from the house in late spring. Set them in the garden or give them away to a friend to put in their garden but never reuse them as house plants. Don't expect the same quantity and quality of blooms in the house as the plants produce outside. Your diligence, however, should be rewarded by the great gift of a rose in bloom in the dark days of December, January and February.

DISPLAYING AND SHOWING YOUR ROSES

Your roses are doing very well and you would like to do more than just enjoy them in your own garden. You may want to bring some flowers into the house to brighten up a room, or you think your friends would enjoy a bouquet. Maybe you want to show off your flowers and compare them to others' blooms at a rose show. Finally, you may want to photograph your flowers so that you can remember and enjoy them when the real ones are gone for the season. Displaying your flowers or photographs of them for yourself and for others, is exciting. Besides giving you a great feeling of pride, displaying your roses in your home or in a show can only help you to grow them better.

CUT FLOWERS IN YOUR HOME

To see a vase of roses in your home—roses that you grew in your garden and look as good, if not better than the best most expensive florist roses—is a source of genuine excitement and pride. That excitement and pride is only equaled by the glow of appreciation on a friend's face when they receive a bouquet of *your* homegrown roses. As with any aspect of rose care, there is a way to handle your cut flowers to give you the best return for your efforts. In other words, long-lasting and good-looking flowers.

The important factors that affect how long your cut flowers will last and how fresh they will look are: the way in which you cut them; limiting the interruption of the water flow from stem to flower; and using clean containers, tools and plenty of fresh water.

When selecting flowers to cut you have to consider what's best for the life of the cut flower and best for the remaining bush. The best time to cut flowers for longer life is in the late afternoon. The sugar content of the leaves and flowers is highest late in the day. Early morning is the next most desirable time. Late morning to mid afternoon is to be avoided.

The stage of flower opening is important also. If the flower bud is too tight the cut flower won't open fully. Flowers can be cut, with no fear of them not opening, any time after the green sepals are reflexed downward and the outer petals are slightly expanded. When cutting clusters of bloom from a floribunda at least one-half of the flowers in the cluster should be at the stage described.

The length at which the stem should be cut is simple. Cut it as if you were cutting away an old bloom. From tall plants you can cut a long stem while with medium and short plants you will have to cut correspondingly shorter stems. This way you always leave the bush neat and clean and ready to bloom again. Lastly, try to cut your flowers from different plants to give continuity of present and successive blooms in the garden.

Obviously, when you cut the flower stems you cut the conductive tissue within the stem that transports water to the flowers. But if you place the lower end of the stem into clean, fresh water immediately, there is little interruption in the capillary action that draws the water up into the flower. This uninterrupted supply of water means that the flower will open fully, the colors will stay clear, the foliage will stay crisp and the neck (right below the flower) will stay straight and erect for almost as long as if the flower remained on the bush. If the cut end is left exposed to the air for any length of time, the conductive tissue, or veins, at the cut end will dry out and collapse, allowing very little water to enter the stem when you do eventually get the stem into water.

When you go out into the garden to cut your flowers always bring a clean bucket of fresh water along. The bucket doesn't have to be full (that can get heavy) but it should have enough water to cover the cut stem ends when you place them in the bucket.

When you arrange your flowers in the house, keep them out of water only briefly. If you give a bouquet to friends, transport it in water. A jar or bucket may not be as elegant as flowers wrapped in paper, but your friends will appreciate those extra days the flowers will last. If impossible to transport them in water, keep the flowers in water until the very last minute before you go. Then wrap them in waxed paper or butcher paper. When you arrive at your destination, cut one inch off the stem ends and place them in warm water up to their necks for an hour to revive them.

Bacteria and dirt on or in anything that comes in contact with the cut flowers will mean limp, short-lived blooms instead of erect, long-lasting flowers. Bacteria grow rapidly if given even slightly favorable conditions and will plug up, like a cork, the conductive tissue at the cut end of the stem limiting the water flowing up to the flowers. Cleanliness is the only thing that keeps bacteria at bay. All your containers should be drinking glass clean. Any knife or shears used should be sharp and clean. Water should always be fresh.

When arranging your flowers remove all thorns and leaves that will be under water in your vase as these act as a breeding ground for bacteria. Pull or rub them off. Never cut them, as you might cut into the stem and cut the conductive tissue. The ends of the stems should be cut on a slant instead of straight across to keep the ends from resting flush on the vase bottom where bacteria and dirt collect. You should also try, if the flowers are not in a very formal arrangement, to recut the stem ends about one-fourth to one-half inch, and completely change the water with cold fresh water, every few days. This added attention adds days to the life of your cut flowers.

Additionally check the water level in your vase daily as you will be amazed how much water a few roses can drink on a warm day. If you receive cut roses either from friends or a florist, use this basic hygiene to make them last longer too.

SHOWING AT A ROSE SHOW

Even if you are mainly interested in growing your roses for your own enjoyment, you can't help but feel pleased when they are admired by others. And what better place to show them off than at a rose show and so have your gardening skills recognized by your peers. You might just experience the excitement and thrill of winning a ribbon or trophy. But even if you don't win anything, it is still fun to participate. You can compare your roses to others, meet and learn from other rose gardeners and see new or different varieties that you may want to try.

Don't think you can't enter or enjoy the show because you have a small garden or are a relative newcomer to rose growing. The first rose we ever grew was an 89 cent, left-over packaged rose bought at a supermarket. The variety was "Peace" and it produced one beautiful flower on a very short stem in time for the Corvallis, Oregon rose show. On the encouragement of a rose-growing friend, we decided to enter it in the show. It was far from perfect but nevertheless won a second place ribbon in the novice "Peace" section. The thrill of winning our ribbon couldn't have been equaled by the top trophy winner of that show.

Organization of a Rose Show

Rose shows are put on by local rose societies of which there are many in the Pacific Northwest. All shows are organized along guidelines set up by the American Rose Society, so they will vary little in organization and rules. They are usually held in June and July with a few scheduled for the late flowering spurt in September. Most are open to all and charge no entry fee. There are novice classes for those of you who have never exhibited before or have exhibited infrequently, as well as sections for ex-perienced gardeners. By virtue of the various classes used, you never have to worry about your roses being judged against those of people who have been growing and exhibiting for a longer time.

The number of rose exhibiting sections, groups of similar roses that are judged against each other, are infinite. They encompass all the rose classification types as well as different colors, flower forms and different varieties. They also include different numbers of flowers within sections and different stages of bloom. There are first, second, and third place ribbons for almost all sections with trophies for outstanding entries. These sections are enumerated in the rose show schedule available before the show from the sponsoring rose society.

No matter in what section a rose is entered, it is judged on the basis of a standard conception of perfection. Flower form, color and substance for any particular variety are deemed most important. Stem and leaves, healthy and in proportion to the flower, are of lesser importance but nevertheless necessary for a good score. Judging is performed by teams of judges, who are amateur gardeners like yourself, and who have attended a special judging school run by the American Rose Society.

After reading the show schedule you may be a little confused and perhaps overwhelmed by all the possibilities. Don't be. What you will enter is decided by three factors: what you are growing, (obviously if you are only growing floribundas you can only enter a floribunda); what you decide beforehand to enter (you may have some new roses that are too young to be cut); and lastly what, due to the caprices of the weather, is available at show time. Choose the roses you want to exhibit first and then find the category they fit into. Don't try to take the show by storm the first time out. The big step is growing at least a few roses that you feel are good enough for the show, exhibiting them, and maybe winning a ribbon.

You *can* show and compete successfully with your roses grown along the lines of the rose care outlined in the seasonal section of this book. But, you can also undertake a few extra chores with your bushes and your show flowers to give you an even better chance of winning a ribbon.

Growing Show Blooms

Garden care to encourage show quality flowers involves some extra spraying and pruning. Spraying your roses every three weeks is usually enough protection for garden enjoyment. But when foliage, stems and flowers have to be close to perfection, you should spray your roses every week to ten days starting at

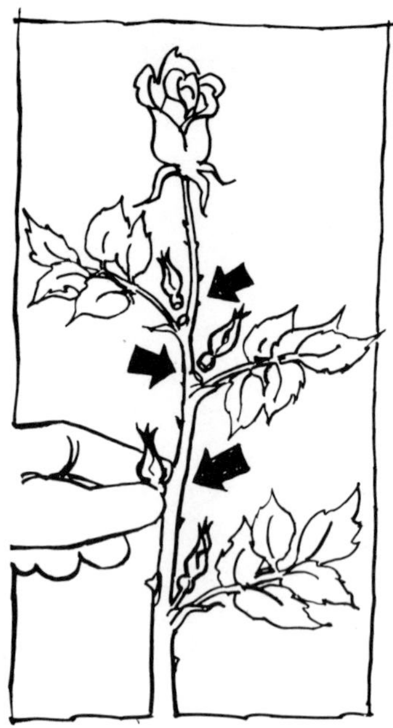

14. Pinch out any secondary tiny flower buds that develop at the leaf-stem junction on single stem roses.

least one and a half months before the show date. Curled, misshapen leaves due to aphids or worms and evidence of mildew or blackspot will detract from your score.

Pruning your roses for the show is easy. The goal is to have one large rose on a single stem for roses entered in the hybrid tea sections, and evenly opened roses in rose clusters entered in the floribunda and other multiple bloom per stem sections.

Almost all naturally grown single stem roses form small side flower buds at the leaf junctions just below the main flower bud. In order to get the maximum size and best appearance on the main flower, you must remove these side buds. This process is called disbudding. Remove the side flower buds as soon as you can see them. Use your fingernails or a small scissors. Remove as much of the tiny bud and stem as possible without breaking the leaf stalk.

The center flower bud of most flower clusters, as on floribundas, will usually open first and be larger than the other buds in the cluster. If you remove this center bud as soon as you can see it, using your fingernails or small scissors, the remaining flowers in the cluster will be larger and open more evenly and so present a much more symmetrical appearance on the show table.

15. Pinch out the large central flower bud of a flower cluster.

Choosing Your Flowers Before the Show

It is the day before the show and you have already decided what sections you want to enter. Now is the time to decide which roses in your garden you are going to subject to the scrutiny of the judges.

Look at your blooms and remember what the judges will be looking for. Form is most important so the flower should have a symmetrical opening of the petals. Try to cut your roses so they will be between one-half to three-fourths open at show time. The center must be well defined. Split or confused centers should not be considered. The color should be clear, strong and sharp for the particular variety. Petals should have substance. Foliage should be green, clean, and well formed with a strong straight stem under the flower or flower cluster.

16. Split or double-centered blooms should not be taken to the rose show.

Any well cared for garden should have a few flowers that fit this description. Some flowers will have a few imperfections, such as a torn leaf or blotch on the outer petal. Cut these latter ones anyway, if you feel they have a chance. Let the judges at the show decide. Besides, only if you bring a flower to the show will you be able to compare it with others and see what you're doing right or wrong.

Cut the stem of the chosen flower or flower cluster as if for the house. All your tools and buckets should be clean and the water fresh. Place the stem in the water immediately. Label the container or stem with the variety name so you don't forget what it is. Cut your roses in the late afternoon of the day before the show and store them overnight in a very cool place such as a garage or basement, in water almost up to their necks. Even if you're content with the flowers you have cut the day before the show, check your bushes on the morning of the show too. A prize winner that wasn't apparent the previous afternoon may have developed overnight.

Grooming Your Flowers at the Show

Before you leave home make sure you have your pruning shears, a small scissors, the show schedule, pen or pencil, a jar of water with a drop or two of dishwashing liquid, and of course your flowers labeled with the variety names.

Most shows accept entries until 10 a.m. with judging taking place between 10 a.m. and noon. Don't be alarmed when you arrive and first catch sight of the staging area. A more confusing mass of people and flowers you are not likely to see. Just look for the rose society members who are ushering. They will help you find vases, water, entry tags and a place to groom your flowers.

First, fill out the entry tags with the variety name, section entered, and your name and address (so the prize committee will know where to send your ribbon). Next place your flowers in the vases with the right entry tags around them. Then give them their final grooming.

Cut out any broken or torn leaves, leaving as many good leaves as possible. Clean the leaves with the soapy water solution and a soft cloth. Commercial oil leaf cleaners are not allowed. Re-cut your stems if necessary to a length that is right for the vase and flowers. Finally bring your entry to the placing table at the door to the exhibiting room. The society members here will check your entry tag, section entered and put the rose on the right table for you.

Whether you brought one rose or many to the show there is little more you can do now to affect the outcome. But there is always next year. Spend some time observing how the other entrants groom their roses. Everyone is excited and pressed for time, but they are all gardeners and are more than happy to share their knowledge about exhibiting roses. They were once just like you—coming to the show with a few roses, not exactly sure what to do and getting a little better at it each time they have returned.

When the show finally opens to the public you may have been lucky and there will be a ribbon around your rose. If not, take time to see who won and why. Not just your own section but other sections, too. Look at what roses took top honors and see how they compare to the others in their sections. Check out any of the speciality exhibits, like new varieties and public garden displays. Finally, whether you've entered a rose or not, go to the show and enjoy the fun and excitement of seeing a beautiful collection of the queen of flowers.

PHOTOGRAPHING YOUR ROSES

Pictures are a wonderful way to look at your roses when the real ones are unavailable. Whether in winter or between flushes of growth in the summer, photographs are a permanent record of your rose growing accomplishments. Besides the sheer joy of just looking at them, photographs can serve some very important practical purposes. When contemplating landscape changes or replacing an older variety during the winter, a picture of the garden or rose planting is better than memory. A photograph of an unknown disease or insect problem can aid in its identification. When visiting public gardens or friends' homes, pictures of rose varieties or new rose landscaping ideas can help you in improving your own grounds. And of course there is nothing like photographs of your flowers to show off to friends to "help" them out, too.

Camera equipment is infinite in variety and you will know best the advantages or limitations of your camera. There are a few techniques to be aware of regardless of camera type that will help you to take very satisfying and useful pictures of your roses and garden.

Light is the first item to think about. Modern films, both color and black and white, are excellent but they don't match the ability of the human eye to see varying degrees of contrast between light and dark. On a very sunny day, for example, the human eye is able to see form and color definition that film cannot duplicate. This fact is very important with roses, as all rose flower color is extremely bright even in low light conditions. In order to get good color photographs of roses you should try to take pictures on a mildly overcast day. The camera will pick up the subtleties of light and dark, giving you good form and color definition on a cloudy-bright day. Early morning or late afternoon on a cloudless day are also good as the light angle from the sun is low producing a softer light. Bright and/or overhead sunlight just increases the high contrast of the roses, leading to a washed-out look in your final photograph. Strong light also produces strong shadows leading to very dark areas in your pictures.

Composition of your pictures is also important. Before you snap the shutter decide what and why you want to photograph. For instance, do you want a closeup of a truly spectacular bloom or do you want a mass of color from a large grouping of roses. Use other garden elements such as a path, tree or fence to frame your pictures and add interest. Don't hesitate to groom your plants by removing the old bloom, for example, to make them look better.

As you photograph roses for whatever purpose, it is a good practice to write down the names of the varieties you are photographing. Flower color has many influences on it, to which you are adding the characteristics of a particular brand of film. You may think you know what you have taken after spending a day at a public garden but when you receive your film or slides, the colors are not quite as you remember them. Matching the pictures to a list is better than matching them to a memory.

Many of the aspects of taking a good photograph are the same qualities that we strive for in creating a garden. The elements of design that you strive for in your picture-taking will help you to develop and sharpen your ability to see new elements in a familiar landscape.

APPENDIX

OUR FAVORITE ROSE VARIETIES

Here is a list of our favorite roses to grow in the Pacific Northwest. They are all commercially available, although not necessarily from the same nursery. Colors are approximate and will differ slightly due to differences in local soils and climate. Check your nearest public rose garden, friends' gardens and catalog description for exact colors and growth habit.

Our roses are divided into the major classifications with an additional list of roses with single, open flowers that are great for naturalizing with other plants and shrubs.

Hybrid Teas and Grandifloras

Duet	Pink
Double Delight	White, pink blend. AARS; City of Portland Gold Award; very fragrant.
Electron	Pink. AARS; City of Portland Gold Award
Fragrant Cloud	Orange-red. AARS; City of Portland Gold Award; very fragrant.
Futura	Orange
Granada	Red, gold blend. AARS.
Gypsy	Red. AARS.
Mr. Lincoln	Deep Red. AARS.
New Day	Yellow
Paradise	Lavender, red blend. AARS.

Pascali	White. AARS; City of Portland Gold Award.
Peace	Yellow, red blend. AARS; City of Portland Gold Award.
Perfume Delight	Pink. AARS; very fragrant.
Princess Margaret	Pink. City of Portland Gold Award.
Prominent	Deep Orange. AARS; City of Portland Gold Award.
Red Devil	Red. City of Portland Gold Award.
Sunblest	Yellow
Whisky Mac	Gold
White Masterpiece	White
Wini Edmunds	Pink and yellow bi-color

Floribundas

Bambi	Pink
Cathedral	Apricot, salmon blend. AARS; City of Portland Gold Award.
Charisma	Orange, gold blend. AARS; City of Portland Gold Award.
Circus	Yellow, pink, scarlet blend. AARS.
City of Belfast	Deep red
Elizabeth of Glamis	Pink
Europeana	Scarlet. AARS; City of Portland Gold Award.
Evening Star	White. City of Portland Gold Award.
Ice White	White. City of Portland Gold Award.
Liverpool Echo	Pink
Razzle-Dazzle	Red and white bi-color. City of Portland Gold Award.
Sunsprite	Yellow
Trumpeter	Scarlet
Winifred Coulter	Red, white blend

Climbers

America	Pink. AARS
Dortmund	Red. City of Portland Gold Award.
Handel	White, pink blend. City of Portland Gold Award.
Joseph's Coat	Orange, red, and yellow blend
Royal Sunset	Gold. City of Portland Gold Award.

Miniatures

Baby Darling	Orange, pink blend
Baby Masquerade	Yellow, red blend
Lavender Lace	Lavender
Magic Carrousel	Red and white bi-color
Shooting Star	Yellow, red blend
Simplex	White
Starina	Orange-scarlet
Yellow Doll	Yellow

Singles for Naturalizing

Dainty Maid	Pink. City of Portland Gold Award.
Eyepaint	Red
Nearly Wild	Pink
Orangeade	Orange. City of Portland Gold Award.
Poulsen's Pearl	Pink
Picasso	Red, white blend
Pinafore	White
Sarabande	Orange, red blend. AARS; City of Portland Gold Award
White Wings	White

IDENTIFICATION OF DISEASES AND INSECTS

Fungus Diseases

Fungus diseases are especially debilitating to roses because they directly attack the leaves. The leaves are where all the food is produced for the plant to maintain and increase its vigor and flower production.

Fungi are chlorophyl-lacking members of the plant kingdom and have to depend on other plants for food. They live by sending their tiny rootlike threads (mycellium) into green and growing plants to extract food from the plant cells. They reproduce by means of tiny spores that spread to other surfaces by wind and water. These spores are very primitive "seeds" and can survive periods of cold and drought.

What you see on the rose leaves is the spore-making part of the fungus. You might think of it as a collection of tiny mushrooms. What you don't see are the tiny mycellium in the leaf itself sapping its strength.

You will also notice that some rose varieties are more susceptible to certain diseases than others. If you have a variety that is infected early in the season and is hard to rid of the disease, you have a carrier, which is a center of infection in your garden. Remove the variety and your disease problems will be reduced.

Disease	Symptoms	Comments
Mildew	Raised white felt, white dust or snow appears on new leaves and new flower buds.	Very severe in warm wet spring and fall, and less troublesome during hot, dry summers. Many new varieties are mildew resistant because of their leathery foliage. Best time to check for mildew resistance in a prospective variety is in October. If it has little or no mildew then, it has good resistance.
Black Spot	Smooth black or brownish-black spots on older leaves.	At the early stages the black spots will be surrounded by the green of the leaf. As it grows, the area around the spots will turn yellow and the leaf will drop off. This disease thrives in hot weather and can spread at a fantastic rate if uncontrolled.
Rust	Raised, small, orange and/or black dots on the underside of the older leaves.	Leaves look yellowed when viewed from above. Rust can defoliate a rose bush very quickly if uncontrolled.

Other Diseases

Disease	Symptoms	Comments
Virus	Leaves have mosaic pattern of irregular green shapes separated by yellow lines or mottled green and orange brown color.	Doesn't spread from plant to plant except by grafting. Unsightly but doesn't bother the vigor of some varieties. There is nothing you can do except complain to the nursery where you bought your plants and ask for a replacement.

Disease	Symptoms	Comments
Crown Gall	Lumpy, bumpy, ridged mound or growth at the crown or bud union of the plant.	A bacterial disease that can seriously weaken your plant. The disease can be spread on tools from plant to plant and in the soil. Never cut into the gall growth on a bush. If you do by accident, dip your shears or loppers in a bleach solution to sterilize them before working on the next plant. Remove any infected plants from your garden. Inspect any new plants —bareroot or potted— for crown gall and do not plant them in your garden if gall is in evidence.

Insects

Insect	Symptoms	Comments
Mites	Leaves look yellow. Underside of older leaves has small white webs and tiny brown spiders.	Mites love hot, dry weather. You may need a magnifying glass to see them.
Aphids	Green, brown, or black oval-shaped insects, can be winged or wingless.	Love tender, new flower buds and new leaves. Aphids usually don't feed on older leaves.
Green worms (caterpillars)	Leaves are curled up and appear to be glued together with white cotton. Holes are chewed in the surrounding leaves.	Worms are at their worst in spring and fall.

Insect	Symptoms	Comments
Cane Borers	Top few inches of cut end of older canes turn brown. Very tiny holes can be seen at the cut end of the stem.	You will probably never see the insect itself. After winter pruning, paint your cuts with pruning compound to prevent damage.
Thrips	Tiny, thin black insects will be seen crawling around flower petals as sepals reflex and flowers unfold.	In severe cases, petals will open up with holes in them.
Spittle Bug	Mass of spit— white and foamy— at the leaf-stem junctions.	Tiny green bug will be hiding inside.
Gall Wasp	Small (about marble size) hairy irregular round growth at upper ends of new canes.	Very rare, and not very serious as the growth is never apparent on more than a few canes.

Leaf Problems

Problem	Symptom	Comments
Hail	Shotgun or BB holes in the leaves.	Very unsightly. You will only see damage in April and May when the Pacific Northwest suffers unstable weather.
Spray damage	Burnt edges on leaves.	Never spray when temperature is over 85°, follow the label dosages and you won't have this problem.

Problem	Symptoms	Comments
Lower Leaf Yellowing	Lower leaves turn an even yellow with no sign of disease and drop off.	Top leaves and canes are using nutrients more efficiently so plant siphons them off from lower shaded leaves.
Deer, Rabbit and Squirrel	New canes will be chewed off.	Fences and repellent are the answers. Problem ceases as canes mature.

Flower Problems

Problem	Symptoms	Comments
Double Centers	Flower opens with 2 centers or a line down the middle of the flower.	Usually occurs in the cool spring when the flower bud develops over a long period. Don't look at the form and just enjoy the color and fragrance.
Blind Shoots (non-flowering canes)	New normal canes that should have a flower bud at their top ends but don't and have stopped growing.	Again this problem is characteristic of cool springs. Cut the top end of the cane off (as if it were a faded flower) and you will promote a new flowering cane from below.
Mushball	Rose flower rots and turns brown as soon as sepals reflex.	You will see this anytime the weather turns wet and cool. It is characteristic of certain rose varieties.

Problem	**Symptoms**	**Comments**
Funny Buds	Flower buds grow bent, lopsided or parallel to the ground. Flowers open and only have a few petals and what appear to be strange leaves coming out of the center of the flower.	These are growth defects that are caused by the speed of spring growth and/or the severe changes in spring and fall weather. They are not symptoms of any serious defect in the rose and by cutting off the damage (like a faded flower) you will promote new canes to grow with perfect flowers.

SOIL TEST LABORATORIES

Soil Test Lab
Oregon State University
Corvallis, OR 97331

Soil Test Lab
Washington State University
Pullman, WA 99163

Provincial Soil Test Lab
B.C. Ministry of Agriculture
1873 Spall Street
Kelowna, B.C.
Canada

PUBLIC ROSE GARDENS IN THE PACIFIC NORTHWEST

Roses are not only popular with home gardeners in this region but with city, state and large private parks as well. There are many excellent parks and gardens with rose plantings open to the public to visit and enjoy. They are pleasant places in which to walk, not only during the summer, but also at any other time of year. They are informative and educational, as you can learn new gardening techniques and see new rose varieties you might want to try at home. By seeing how different varieties grow in these gardens you can see exactly what the colors and habit of the plants will be in your garden.

There are two All-America Rose Selection (AARS) official test gardens in our area. AARS conducts a rose testing program whose goal is to pick outstanding roses for the home gardener. Each year four plants of approximately 40 entries are sent out by member rose firms to 26 public gardens around the country. These roses are grown under a code number for a two-year testing period. They are judged for habit, form, color, disease resistance and flower production. Each year only two or three varieties are selected to receive the AARS award. At the Portland and Seattle gardens you can see both the coded entries and the recent AARS winners. In addition, most of the other gardens listed feature the new AARS winners.

There is an American Rose Society Miniature Rose Test Garden in Portland which conducts a similar program to AARS but only for minis. The city of Portland also gives a Gold Award each year (the only city in North America to do so) to outstanding roses that have grown particularly well in the Pacific Northwest. A special section of the Portland garden is reserved for Gold Award winners.

Take advantage of these gardens for their beauty and information whenever you are near one. Here is a list of the best in the Northwest.

Washington

Fairhaven Park Rose Garden
108 Chuckanut Drive
Bellingham, WA 98225

1,000 Roses

Chehalis Municipal Rose Garden
80 N.E. Cascade
Chehalis, WA 98532

500 Roses

Woodland Park Rose Garden
700 North 50th Street
Seattle, WA 98103

5,000 Roses
AARS Test Garden

Rose Hill
Manito Park
West 4-21st Avenue
Spokane, WA 99203

2,200 Roses

Point Defiance Park Rose Garden
5402 North Shirley
Tacoma, WA 98407

3,500 Roses

Oregon

Shore Acres State Park
Route 2
Coos Bay, OR 97420

1,000 Roses

Corvallis Rose Garden
Avery Park
South 15th Street
Corvallis, OR 97330

1,500 Roses

Municipal Rose Garden   3,500 Roses
3 North Jefferson
Eugene, Or 97401

Jackson and Perkins Test Garden   1,500 Roses
2518 South Pacific Highway
Medford, OR 97501

International Rose Test Garden   8,000 Roses, AARS Test
400 S.W. Kingston   Garden, ARS Miniature
Portland, OR 97201   Test Garden, City of
                                              Portland Gold Award
                                              Garden

Peninsula Park Rose Garden   10,000 Roses
6400 North Albina
Portland, OR 97217

Bush's Pasture Park
Mission and High Streets
Salem, OR 97301

British Columbia

University of British Columbia   1,000 Roses
Rose Garden
The Botanical Garden
University of British Columbia
Vancouver B.C.
Canada VGT 1W5

Park and Tilford Gardens   1,500 Roses
1240 Cotton
North Vancouver B.C.
Canada

The Butchart Gardens   2,000 Roses
800 Benvenuto
Victoria B.C.
Canada

PACIFIC NORTHWEST ROSE NURSERIES

Pacific Northwesterners are particularly fortunate in having a number of very fine rose growers and rose nurseries in the region. They are all a pleasure to do business with and are only too glad to send you a catalog.

Jackson and Perkins
P.O. Box 1028
Medford, OR 97501

Roses by Fred Edmunds
6235 S.W. Kahle Road
Wilsonville, OR 97070

Roseway Nursery
8766 N.E. Sandy Blvd.
Portland, OR 97220

Small World Miniatures
P.O. Box 562
Rogue River, OR 97527

United Rose Growers
1531 Guild Road, P.O. Box E-1
Woodland, WA 98674

Windy Hill Miniature Roses
5947 S.W. Kahle Road
Wilsonville, OR 97070

YOUR LOCAL ROSE SOCIETY

There are 20 local rose societies affiliated with the American Rose Society in the Pacific Northwest. They are groups of amateur gardeners, like yourself, who share a deep interest in growing roses. They organize rose shows every spring and fall to exhibit roses.The societies also hold monthly meetings on different gardening topics with speakers from all over the Pacific Northwest.

The American Rose Society also has a program of Consulting Rosarians to help people with their rose problems. Consulting Rosarians are members of a local rose society, who have grown roses for many years and want to share that knowledge with others. These people are more than willing to help you with your rose problems at no cost to you.

For the address of your local rose society and Consulting Rosarians in your area, you can write to:

American Rose Society
Box 30,000
Shreveport, LA 71130

INDEX